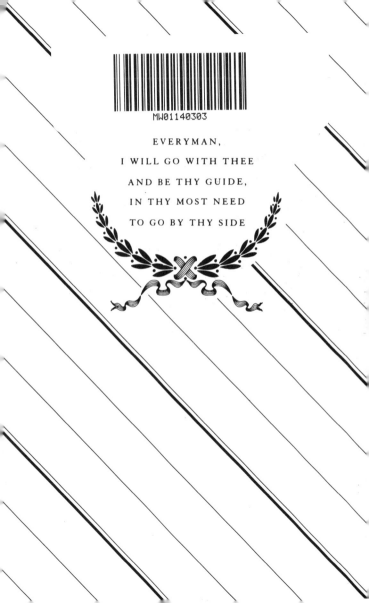

EVERYMAN,
I WILL GO WITH THEE
AND BE THY GUIDE,
IN THY MOST NEED
TO GO BY THY SIDE

EVERYMAN'S LIBRARY
POCKET POETS

PUSHKIN

EUGENE ONEGIN
AND OTHER POEMS

TRANSLATED BY
CHARLES JOHNSTON

EVERYMAN'S LIBRARY
POCKET POETS

Alfred A. Knopf New York London Toronto

THIS IS A BORZOI BOOK
PUBLISHED BY ALFRED A. KNOPF

First published in Everyman's Library, 1999
This translation of *Eugene Onegin* first published 1977; revised 1979
Copyright © Charles Johnston, 1977, 1979
Published by arrangement with Penguin UK Ltd. All rights reserved.
'Onegin's Journey' and 'The Bronze Horseman' from *Narrative Poems by
Alexander Pushkin and Mikhail Lermontov*, translated by Charles Johnston.
Copyright © 1979, 1980, 1982, 1983 by Charles Johnston
Reprinted in the US by permission of Random House, Inc. and
in the UK by permission of The Bodley Head, London.

Sixth printing (US)

All rights reserved. Published in the United States by Alfred A. Knopf,
a division of Random House, Inc., New York, and in Canada by Random
House of Canada Limited, Toronto. Distributed by Random House, Inc.,
New York. Published in the United Kingdom by Everyman's Library,
Northburgh House, 10 Northburgh Street, London EC1V 0AT.
Distributed by Random House (UK) Ltd.

US website: www.randomhouse.com/everymans

ISBN 978-0-375-40672-0 (US)
978-1-85715-739-0 (UK)

A CIP catalogue record for this book is available from the British Library

Typography by Peter B. Willberg

Typeset in the UK by AccComputing, North Barrow, Somerset
Printed and bound in Germany by GGP Media GmbH, Pössneck

ALEXANDER PUSHKIN

EUGENE
ONEGIN

Pétri de vanité, il avait encore plus de cette espèce d'orgueil qui fait avouer avec la même indifférence les bonnes comme les mauvaises actions, suite d'un sentiment de supériorité peut-être imaginaire.

(Tiré d'une lettre particulière)

Heedless of the proud world's enjoyment,
I prize the attention of my friends,
and only wish that my employment
could have been turned to worthier ends –
worthier of you in the perfection
your soul displays, in holy dreams,
in simple but sublime reflection,
in limpid verse that lives and gleams.
But, as it is, this pied collection
begs your indulgence – it's been spun
from threads both sad and humoristic,
themes popular or idealistic,
products of carefree hours, of fun,
of sleeplessness, faint inspirations,
of powers unripe, or on the wane,
of reason's icy intimations,
and records of a heart in pain.

A Note on the Text

Stanzas omitted or discarded by Pushkin are denoted by roman numerals in parentheses. Discarded text reinstated in this edition is enclosed in square brackets.

CHAPTER ONE

To live, it hurries, and to feel it hastes.

PRINCE VYAZEMSKY

I

'My uncle – high ideals inspire him;
but when past joking he fell sick,
he really forced one to admire him –
and never played a shrewder trick.
Let others learn from his example!
But God, how deadly dull to sample
sickroom attendance night and day
and never stir a foot away!
And the sly baseness, fit to throttle,
of entertaining the half-dead:
one smooths the pillows down in bed,
and glumly serves the medicine bottle,
and sighs, and asks oneself all through:
"When will the devil come for you?"'

II

Such were a young rake's meditations –
by will of Zeus, the high and just,
the legatee of his relations –
as horses whirled him through the dust.
Friends of my Ruslan and Lyudmila,
without preliminary feeler
let me acquaint you on the nail
with this the hero of my tale:
Onegin, my good friend, was littered
and bred upon the Neva's brink,
where you were born as well, I think,
reader, or where you've shone and glittered!
There once I too strolled back and forth:
but I'm allergic to the North ...

III

After a fine career, his father
had only debts on which to live.
He gave three balls a year, and rather
promptly had nothing left to give.
Fate saved Evgeny from perdition:
at first Madame gave him tuition,
from her Monsieur took on the child.
He was sweet-natured, and yet wild.
Monsieur l'Abbé, the mediocre,
reluctant to exhaust the boy,
treated his lessons as a ploy.
No moralizing from this joker;
a mild rebuke was his worst mark,
and then a stroll in Letny Park.

IV

But when the hour of youthful passion
struck for Evgeny, with its play
of hope and gloom, romantic-fashion,
it was goodbye, Monsieur l'Abbé.
Eugene was free, and as a dresser
made London's *dandy* his professor.
His hair was fashionably curled,
and now at last he saw the World.
In French Onegin had perfected
proficiency to speak and write,
in the mazurka he was light,
his bow was wholly unaffected.
The World found this enough to treat
Eugene as clever, and quite sweet.

V

We all meandered through our schooling
haphazard; so, to God be thanks,
it's easy, without too much fooling,
to pass for cultured in our ranks.
Onegin was assessed by many
(critical judges, strict as any)
as well-read, though of pedant cast.
Unforced, as conversation passed,
he had the talent of saluting
felicitously every theme,
of listening like a judge-supreme
while serious topics were disputing,
or, with an epigram-surprise,
of kindling smiles in ladies' eyes.

VI

Now Latin's gone quite out of favour;
yet, truthfully and not in chaff,
Onegin knew enough to savour
the meaning of an epigraph,
make Juvenal his text, or better
add *vale* when he signed a letter;
stumblingly call to mind he did
two verses of the Aeneid.
He lacked the slightest predilection
for raking up historic dust
or stirring annalistic must;
but groomed an anecdote-collection
that stretched from Romulus in his prime
across the years to our own time.

VII

He was without that dithyrambic
frenzy which wrecks our lives for sound,
and telling trochee from iambic
was quite beyond his wit, we found.
He cursed Theocritus and Homer,
in Adam Smith was his diploma;
our deep economist had got
the gift of recognizing what
a nation's wealth is, what augments it,
and how a country lives, and why
it needs no gold if a supply
of *simple product* supplements it.
His father failed to understand
and took a mortgage on his land.

VIII

Evgeny's total store of knowledge
I have no leisure to recall;
where he was master of his college,
the art he'd studied best of all,
his young heyday's supreme employment,
its work, its torture, its enjoyment,
what occupied his chafing powers
throughout the boredom of the hours –
this was the science of that passion
which Ovid sang, for which the bard,
condemned to a lifetime of hard,
ended his wild career of fashion
deep in Moldavia the abhorred,
far, far from Italy, his adored.

(IX) X

How early he'd learnt to dissemble,
to hide a hope, to make a show
of jealousy, to seem to tremble
or pine, persuade of yes or no,
and act the humble or imperious,
the indifferent, or the deadly serious!
In languid silence, or the flame
of eloquence, and just the same
in casual letters of confession –
one thing inspired his breath, his heart,
and self-oblivion was his art!
How soft his glance, or at discretion
how bold or bashful there, and here
how brilliant with its instant tear!

XI

How well he donned new shapes and sizes –
startling the ingenuous with a jest,
frightening with all despair's disguises,
amusing, flattering with the best,
stalking the momentary weakness,
with passion and with shrewd obliqueness
swaying the artless, waiting on
for unmeant kindness – how he shone!
then he'd implore a declaration,
and listen for the heart's first sound,
pursue his love – and at one bound
secure a secret assignation,
then afterwards, alone, at ease,
impart such lessons as you please!

XII

How early on he learnt to trouble
the heart of the professional flirt!
When out to burst a rival's bubble,
how well he knew the way to hurt –
what traps he'd set him, with what malice
he'd pop the poison in his chalice!
But you, blest husbands, to the end
you kept your friendship with our friend:
the subtle spouse was just as loyal –
Faublas' disciple for an age –
as was the old suspicious sage,
and the majestic, antlered royal,
always contented with his life,
and with his dinner, and his wife.

(XIII, XIV,) XV

Some days he's still in bed, and drowses,
when little notes come on a tray
What? Invitations? Yes, three houses
have each asked him to a soirée:
a ball here, there a children's party;
where shall he go, my rogue, my hearty?
Which one comes first? It's just the same –
to do them all is easy game.
Meanwhile, attired for morning strolling
complete with broad-brimmed bolivar,
Eugene attends the boulevard,
and there at large he goes patrolling
until Bréguet's unsleeping chime
advises him of dinner-time.

XVI

He mounts the sledge, with daylight fading:
'Make way, make way,' goes up the shout;
his collar in its beaver braiding
glitters with hoar-frost all about.
He's flown to Talon's, calculating
that there his friend Kavérin's waiting;
he arrives – the cork goes flying up,
wine of the Comet fills the cup;
before him roast beef, red and gory,
and truffles, which have ever been
youth's choice, the flower of French cuisine;
and pâté, Strasbourg's deathless glory,
sits with Limburg's vivacious cheese
and *ananas*, the gold of trees.

XVII

More wine, he calls, to drench the flaming
fire of the cutlets' scalding fat,
when Bréguet's chime is heard proclaiming
the new ballet he should be at.
He's off – this ruthless legislator
for the footlights, this fickle traitor
to all the most adored *actrices*,
this denizen of the *coulisses*
that world where every man's a critic
who'll clap an *entrechat*, or scoff
at Cleopatra, hiss her off,
boo Phaedra out as paralytic,
encore Moëna, – and rejoice
to know the audience hears his voice.

XVIII

Enchanted land! There like a lampion
that king of the satiric scene,
Fonvizin sparkled, freedom's champion,
and the derivative Knyazhnín:
there Ózerov shared the unwilling
tribute of tears, applause's shrilling,
with young Semyónova, and there
our friend Katénin brought to bear
once more Corneille's majestic story;
there caustic Shakhovskóy came in
with comedies of swarm and din;
there Didelot crowned himself with glory:
there, where the *coulisse* entrance went,
that's where my years of youth were spent.

XIX

My goddesses! Where are you banished?
lend ears to my lugubrious tone:
have other maidens, since you vanished,
taken your place, though not your throne?
your chorus, is it dead for ever?
Russia's Terpsichore, shall never
again I see your soulful flight?
shall my sad gaze no more alight
on features known, but to that dreary,
that alien scene must I now turn
my disillusioned glass, and yearn,
bored with hilarity, and weary,
and yawn in silence at the stage
as I recall a bygone age?

XX

The house is packed out; scintillating,
the boxes; boiling, pit and stalls;
the gallery claps – it's bored with waiting –
and up the rustling curtain crawls.
Then with a half-ethereal splendour,
bound where the magic bow will send her,
Istómina, thronged all around
by Naiads, one foot on the ground,
twirls the other slowly as she pleases,
then suddenly she's off, and there
she's up and flying through the air
like fluff before Aeolian breezes;
she'll spin this way and that, and beat
against each other swift, small feet.

XXI

Applause. Onegin enters – passes
across the public's toes; he steers
straight to his stall, then turns his glasses
on unknown ladies in the tiers;
he's viewed the boxes without passion,
he's seen it all; with looks and fashion
he's dreadfully dissatisfied;
to gentlemen on every side
he's bowed politely; his attention
wanders in a distracted way
across the stage; he yawns: 'Ballet –
they all have richly earned a pension;'
he turns away: 'I've had enough –
now even Didelot's tedious stuff.'

XXII

Still tumbling, devil, snake and Cupid
on stage are thumping without cease;
still in the porch, exhausted-stupid,
the footmen sleep on the *pelisses*;
the audience still is busy stamping,
still coughing, hissing, clapping, champing;
still everywhere the lamps are bright;
outside and in they star the night;
still shivering in the bitter weather
the horses fidget worse and worse;
the coachmen ring the fire, and curse
their lords, and thwack their palms together;
but Eugene's out from din and press:
by now he's driving home to dress.

XXIII

Shall I depict with expert knowledge
the cabinet behind the door
where the prize-boy of fashion's college
is dressed, undressed, and dressed once more?
Whatever for caprice of spending
ingenious London has been sending
across the Baltic in exchange
for wood and tallow; all the range
of useful objects that the curious
Parisian taste invents for one –
for friends of languor, or of fun,
or for the modishly luxurious –
all this, at eighteen years of age,
adorned the sanctum of our sage.

XXIV

Porcelain and bronzes on the table,
with amber pipes from Tsaregrad;
such crystalled scents as best are able
to drive the swooning senses mad;
with combs, and steel utensils serving
as files, and scissors straight and curving,
brushes on thirty different scales;
brushes for teeth, brushes for nails.
Rousseau (forgive a short distraction)
could not conceive how solemn Grimm
dared clean his nails in front of *him*,
the brilliant crackpot: this reaction
shows freedom's advocate, that strong
champion of rights, as in the wrong.

XXV

A man who's active and incisive
can yet keep nail-care much in mind:
why fight what's known to be decisive?
custom is despot of mankind.
Dressed like [– – –], duly dreading
the barbs that envy's always spreading,
Eugene's a pedant in his dress,
in fact a thorough fop, no less.
Three whole hours, at the least accounting,
he'll spend before the looking-glass,
then from his cabinet he'll pass
giddy as Venus when she's mounting
a masculine disguise to aid
her progress at the masquerade.

XXVI

Your curiosity is burning
to hear what latest modes require,
and so, before the world of learning,
I could describe here his attire;
and though to do so would be daring,
it's my profession; he was wearing –
but *pantaloons*, *waistcoat*, and *frock*,
these words are not of Russian stock:
I know (and seek your exculpation)
that even so my wretched style
already tends too much to smile
on words of foreign derivation,
though years ago I used to look
at the Academic Diction-book.

XXVII

That isn't our immediate worry:
we'd better hasten to the ball,
where, in a cab, and furious hurry,
Onegin has outrun us all.
Along the fronts of darkened houses,
along the street where slumber drowses,
twin lamps of serried coupés throw
a cheerful glimmer on the snow
and radiate a rainbow: blazing
with lampions studded all about
the sumptuous palais shines out;
shadows that flit behind the glazing
project in silhouette the tops
of ladies and of freakish fops.

XXVIII

Up to the porch our hero's driven;
in, past concierge, up marble stair
flown like an arrow, then he's given
a deft arrangement to his hair,
and entered. Ballroom overflowing . . .
and band already tired of blowing,
while a mazurka holds the crowd;
and everything is cramped and loud;
spurs of Chevalier Gardes are clinking,
dear ladies' feet fly past like hail,
and on their captivating trail
incendiary looks are slinking,
while roar of violins contrives
to drown the hiss of modish wives.

XXIX

In days of carefree aspirations,
the ballroom drove me off my head:
the safest place for declarations,
and where most surely notes are sped.
You husbands, deeply I respect you!
I'm at your service to protect you;
now pay attention, I beseech,
and take due warning from my speech.
You too, mamas, I pray attend it,
and watch your daughters closer yet,
yes, focus on them your lorgnette,
or else . . . or else, may God forfend it!
I only write like this, you know,
since I stopped sinning years ago.

XXX

Alas, on pleasure's wild variety
I've wasted too much life away!
But, did they not corrupt society,
I'd still like dances to this day:
the atmosphere of youth and madness,
the crush, the glitter and the gladness,
the ladies' calculated dress;
I love their feet – though I confess
that all of Russia can't contribute
three pairs of handsome ones – yet there
exists for me one special pair!
one pair! I pay them memory's tribute
though cold I am and sad; in sleep
the heartache that they bring lies deep.

XXXI

Oh, when, and to what desert banished,
madman, can you forget their print?
my little feet, where have you vanished,
what flowers of spring display your dint?
Nursed in the orient's languid weakness,
across our snows of northern bleakness
you left no steps that could be tracked:
you loved the opulent contact
of rugs, and carpets' rich refinement.
Was it for you that I became
long since unstirred by praise and fame
and fatherland and grim confinement?
The happiness of youth is dead,
just like, on turf, your fleeting tread.

XXXII

Diana's breast, the cheeks of Flora,
all these are charming! but to put
it frankly, I'm a firm adorer
of the Terpsichorean foot.
It fascinates by its assurance
of recompense beyond endurance,
and fastens, like a term of art,
the wilful fancies of the heart.
My love for it is just as tender,
under the table's linen shield,
on springtime grasses of the field,
in winter, on the cast-iron fender,
on ballroom's looking-glass parquet
or on the granite of the bay.

XXXIII

On the seashore, with storm impending,
how envious was I of the waves
each in tumultuous turn descending
to lie down at her feet like slaves!
I longed, like every breaker hissing,
to smother her dear feet with kissing.
No, never in the hottest fire
of boiling youth did I desire
with any torture so exquisite
to kiss Armida's lips, or seek
the flaming roses of a cheek,
or languid bosoms; and no visit
of raging passion's surge and roll
ever so roughly rocked my soul!

XXXIV

Another page of recollection:
sometimes, in reverie's sacred land,
I grasp a stirrup with affection,
I feel a small foot in my hand;
fancies once more are hotly bubbling,
once more that touch is fiercely troubling
the blood within my withered heart,
once more the love, once more the smart . . .
But, now I've praised the queens of fashion,
enough of my loquacious lyre:
they don't deserve what they inspire
in terms of poetry or passion –
their looks and language in deceit
are just as nimble as their feet.

XXXV

And Eugene? half-awake, half-drowsing,
from ball to bed behold him come;
while Petersburg's already rousing,
untirable, at sound of drum:
the merchant's up, the cabman's walking
towards his stall, the pedlar's hawking;
see with their jugs the milk-girls go
and crisply crunch the morning snow.
The city's early sounds awake her;
shutters are opened and the soft
blue smoke of chimneys goes aloft,
and more than once the German baker,
punctilious in his cotton cap,
has opened up his serving-trap.

XXXVI

Exhausted by the ballroom's clamour,
converting morning to midnight,
he sleeps, away from glare and glamour,
this child of luxury and delight.
Then, after midday he'll be waking;
his life till dawn's already making,
always monotonously gay,
tomorrow just like yesterday.
But was it happy, his employment,
his freedom, in his youth's first flower,
with brilliant conquests by the shower,
and every day its own enjoyment?
Was it to no effect that he,
at feasts, was strong and fancy-free?

XXXVII

No, early on his heart was cooling
and he was bored with social noise;
no, not for long were belles the ruling
objective of his thoughts and joys:
soon, infidelity proved cloying,
and friends and friendship, soul-destroying;
not every day could he wash down
his beefsteak with champagne, or drown
his Strasbourg pie, or point a moral,
full of his usual pith and wit,
with cranium aching fit to split;
and though he liked a fiery quarrel –
yet he fell out of love at last
with sabre's slash, and bullet's blast.

XXXVIII

The illness with which he'd been smitten
should have been analysed when caught,
something like *spleen*, that scourge of Britain,
or Russia's *chondria*, for short;
it mastered him in slow gradation;
thank God, he had no inclination
to blow his brains out, but in stead
to life grew colder than the dead.
So, like Childe Harold, glum, unpleasing,
he stalked the drawing-rooms, remote
from Boston's cloth or gossip's quote;
no glance so sweet, no sigh so teasing,
no, nothing caused his heart to stir,
and nothing pierced his senses' blur.

(XXXIX, XL, XLI,) XLII

Capricious belles of grand Society!
you were the first ones he forswore;
for in our time, beyond dubiety,
the highest circles are a bore.
It's true, I'll not misrepresent them,
some ladies preach from Say and Bentham,
but by and large their talk's a hash
of the most harmless, hopeless trash.
And what's more, they're so supercilious,
so pure, so spotless through and through,
so pious, and so clever too,
so circumspect, and so punctilious,
so virtuous that, no sooner seen,
at once they give a man the spleen.

XLIII

You too, prime beauties in your flower
who late at night are whirled away
by drozhkies jaunting at full power
over the Petersburg *pavé*—
he ended even your employment;
and in retreat from all enjoyment
locked himself up inside his den
and with a yawn took up his pen,
and tried to write, but a hard session
of work made him feel sick, and still
no word came flowing from his quill;
he failed to join that sharp profession
which I myself won't praise or blame
since I'm a member of the same.

XLIV

Idle again by dedication,
oppressed by emptiness of soul,
he strove to achieve the appropriation
of other's thought – a splendid goal;
with shelves of books deployed for action,
he read, and read – no satisfaction:
here's boredom, madness or pretence,
here there's no conscience, here no sense;
they're all chained up in different fetters,
the ancients have gone stiff and cold,
the moderns rage against the old.
He'd given up girls – now gave up letters,
and hid the bookshelf's dusty stack
in taffeta of mourning black.

XLV

Escaped from social rhyme and reason,
retired, as he, from fashion's stream,
I was Onegin's friend that season.
I liked his quality, the dream
which held him silently subjected,
his strangeness, wholly unaffected,
his mind, so cold and so precise.
The bitterness was mine – the ice
was his; we'd both drunk passion's chalice:
our lives were flat, and what had fired
both hearts to blaze had now expired;
there waited for us both the malice
of blind Fortuna and of men
in lives that were just dawning then.

XLVI

He who has lived and thought is certain
to scorn the men with whom he deals;
days that are lost behind the curtain,
ghostlike, must trouble him who feels –
for him all sham has found rejection,
he's gnawed by serpent Recollection,
and by Repentance. All this lends,
on most occasions between friends,
a great attraction to conversing.
At first Onegin's tongue produced
a haze in me, but I grew used
to his disputing and his cursing;
his virulence that made you smile,
his epigrams topped up with bile.

XLVII

How often, when the sky was glowing,
by Neva, on a summer night,
and when its waters were not showing,
in their gay glass, the borrowed light
of Dian's visage, in our fancies
recalling earlier time's romances,
recalling earlier loves, did we,
now sensitive, and now carefree,
drink in the midnight benediction,
the silence when our talk had ceased!
Like convicts in a dream released
from gaol to greenwood, by such fiction
we were swept off, in reverie's haze,
to the beginning of our days.

XLVIII

Evgeny stood, with soul regretful,
and leant upon the granite shelf;
he stood there, pensive and forgetful,
just as the Poet paints himself.
Silence was everywhere enthralling;
just sentries to each other calling,
and then a drozhky's clopping sound
from Million Street came floating round;
and then a boat, with oars a-swinging,
swam on the river's dreaming face,
and then, with an enchanting grace,
came distant horns, and gallant singing.
Yet sweeter far, at such a time,
the strain of Tasso's octave-rhyme!

XLIX

O Adrian waves, my invocation;
O Brenta, I'll see you in dream;
hear, once more filled with inspiration,
the magic voices of your stream,
sacred to children of Apollo!
Proud Albion's lyre is what I follow,
through it they're known to me, and kin.
Italian nights, when I'll drink in
your molten gold, your charmed infusion;
with a Venetian maiden who
can chatter, and be silent too,
I'll float in gondola's seclusion;
from her my lips will learn and mark
the tongue of love and of Petrarch.

L

When comes my moment to untether?
'it's time!' and freedom hears my hail.
I walk the shore, I watch the weather,
I signal to each passing sail.
Beneath storm's vestment, on the seaway,
battling along that watery freeway,
when shall I start on my escape?
It's time to drop astern the shape
of the dull shores of my disfavour,
and there, beneath your noonday sky,
my Africa, where waves break high,
to mourn for Russia's gloomy savour,
land where I learned to love and weep,
land where my heart is buried deep.

LI

Eugene would willingly have started
with me to see an alien strand;
but soon the ways we trod were parted
for quite a while by fortune's hand.
His father died; and (as expected)
before Onegin there collected
the usurers' voracious tribe.
To private tastes we each subscribe:
Evgeny, hating litigation,
and satisfied with what he'd got,
made over to them his whole lot,
finding in that no deprivation –
or else, from far off, he could see
old Uncle's end was soon to be.

LII

In fact one day a note came flying
from the agent, with this tale to tell:
Uncle, in bed, and near to dying,
wished him to come and say farewell.
Evgeny read the sad epistle
and set off prompter than a whistle
as fast as post-horses could go,
already yawned before the show,
exercised, under lucre's banner,
in sighs and boredom and deceits
(my tale's beginning here repeats);
but, when he'd rushed to Uncle's manor,
a corpse on boards was all he found,
an offering ready for the ground.

LIII

The yard was bursting with dependants;
there gathered at the coffin-side
friends, foes, priests, guests, inured attendants
of every funeral far and wide;
they buried Uncle, congregated
to eat and drink, then separated
with grave goodbyes to the bereaved,
as if some goal had been achieved.
Eugene turned countryman. He tasted
the total ownership of woods,
mills, lands and waters – he whose goods
till then had been dispersed and wasted –
and glad he was he'd thus arranged
for his old courses to be changed.

LIV

It all seemed new – for two days only –
the coolness of the sombre glade,
the expanse of fields, so wide, so lonely,
the murmur where the streamlet played . . .
the third day, wood and hill and grazing
gripped him no more; soon they were raising
an urge to sleep; soon, clear as clear,
he saw that, as in cities, here
boredom has just as sure an entry,
although there are no streets, no cards,
no mansions, no ballrooms, no bards.
Yes, spleen was waiting like a sentry,
and dutifully shared his life
just like a shadow, or a wife.

LV

No, *I* was born for peace abounding
and country stillness: there the lyre
has voices that are more resounding,
poetic dreams, a brighter fire.
To harmless idleness devoted,
on waves of *far niente* floated,
I roam by the secluded lake.
And every morning I awake
to freedom, softness and enjoyment:
sleep much, read little, and put down
the thought of volatile renown.
Was it not in such sweet employment
such shadowy and leisured ways,
that once I spent my happiest days?

LVI

O flowers, and love, and rustic leisure,
o fields – to you I'm vowed at heart.
I regularly take much pleasure
in showing how to tell apart
myself and Eugene, lest a reader
of mocking turn, or else a breeder
of calculated slander should,
spying my features, as he could,
put back the libel on the table
that, like proud Byron, I can draw
self-portraits only – furthermore
the charge that poets are unable
to sing of others must imply
the poet's only theme is 'I'.

LVII

Poets, I'll say in this connection,
adore the love that comes in dream.
In time past, objects of affection
peopled my sleep, and to their theme
my soul in secret gave survival;
then from the Muse there came revival:
my carefree song would thus reveal
the mountain maiden, my ideal,
and captive girls, by Salgir lying.
And now, my friends, I hear from you
a frequent question: 'tell me who
inspires your lute to sounds of sighing?
To whom do you, from all the train
of jealous girls, devote its strain?

LVIII

'Whose glance, provoking inspiration,
rewards the music of your mind
with fond caress? whose adoration
is in your poetry enshrined?'
No one's, I swear by God! in sadness
I suffered once from all the madness
of love's anxiety. Blessed is he
who can combine it with the free
fever of rhyme: thereby he's doubled
poetry's sacred frenzy, made
a stride on Petrarch's path, allayed
the pangs with which his heart was troubled,
and, with it, forced renown to come –
but I, in love, was dull and dumb.

LIX

Love passed, the Muse appeared, the weather
of mind got clarity new-found;
now free, I once more weave together
emotion, thought, and magic sound;
I write, my heart has ceased its pining,
my thoughtless pen has stopped designing,
beside unfinished lines, a suite
of ladies' heads, and ladies' feet;
dead ash sets no more sparks a-flying;
I'm grieving still, but no more tears,
and soon, oh soon the storm's arrears
will in my soul be hushed and dying.
That's when I'll sit down to compose
an ode in twenty-five cantos.

LX

I've drawn a plan and a projection,
the hero's name's decided too.
Meanwhile my novel's opening section
is finished, and I've looked it through
meticulously; in my fiction
there's far too much of contradiction,
but I refuse to chop or change.
The censor's tribute, I'll arrange;
I'll feed the journalists for dinner
fruits of my labour and my ink . . .
So now be off to Neva's brink,
you newborn work, and like a winner
earn for me the rewards of fame –
misunderstanding, noise, and blame!

CHAPTER TWO

O rus!

HORACE

O Russia!

I

The place where Eugene loathed his leisure
was an enchanting country nook:
there any friend of harmless pleasure
would bless the form his fortune took.
The manor house, in deep seclusion,
screened by a hill from storm's intrusion,
looked on a river: far away
before it was the golden play
of light that flowering fields reflected:
villages flickered far and near,
and cattle roamed the plain, and here
a park, enormous and neglected,
spread out its shadow all around –
the pensive Dryads' hiding-ground.

II

The *château* was of a construction
befitting such a noble pile:
it stood, defiant of destruction
in sensible old-fashioned style.
High ceilings everywhere abounded;
in the saloon, brocade-surrounded,
ancestral portraits met the view
and stoves with tiles of various hue.
All this has now gone out of fashion,
I don't know why, but for my friend
interior décor in the end
excited not a hint of passion:
a modish taste, a dowdy touch –
both set him yawning just as much.

III

The rustic sage, in that apartment,
forty years long would criticise
his housekeeper and her department,
look through the pane, and squash the flies.
Oak-floored, and simple as a stable:
two cupboards, one divan, a table,
no trace of ink, no spots, no stains.
And of the cupboards, one contains
a book of household calculations,
the other, jugs of applejack,
fruit liqueurs and an Almanack
for 1808: his obligations
had left the squire no time to look
at any other sort of book.

IV

Alone amid all his possessions,
to pass the time was Eugene's theme:
it led him, in these early sessions,
to institute a new regime.
A thinker in a desert mission,
he changed the *corvée* of tradition
into a small quit-rent – and got
his serfs rejoicing at their lot.
But, in a fearful huff, his thrifty
neighbour was sure, from this would flow
consequences of hideous woe;
another's grin was sly and shifty,
but all concurred that, truth to speak,
he was a menace, and a freak.

V

At first they called; but on perceiving
invariably, as time went on,
that from the backdoor he'd be leaving
on a fast stallion from the Don,
once on the highway he'd detected
the noise their rustic wheels projected –
they took offence at this, and broke
relations off, and never spoke.
'The man's a boor; his brain is missing,
he's a freemason too; for him,
red wine in tumblers to the brim –
but ladies' hands are not for kissing;
it's *yes* or *no*, but never *sir*.'
The vote was passed without demur.

VI

Meanwhile another new landowner
came driving to his country seat,
and, in the district, this *persona*
drew scrutiny no less complete –
Vladimir Lensky, whose creator
was Göttingen, his *alma mater*,
good-looking, in the flower of age,
a poet, and a Kantian sage.
He'd brought back all the fruits of learning
from German realms of mist and steam,
freedom's enthusiastic dream,
a spirit strange, a spirit burning,
an eloquence of fevered strength,
and raven curls of shoulder-length.

VII

He was too young to have been blighted
by the cold world's corrupt finesse;
his soul still blossomed out, and lighted
at a friend's word, a girl's caress.
In heart's affairs, a sweet beginner,
he fed on hope's deceptive dinner;
the world's *éclat*, its thunder-roll,
still captivated his young soul.
He sweetened up with fancy's icing
the uncertainties within his heart;
for him, the objective on life's chart
was still mysterious and enticing –
something to rack his brains about,
suspecting wonders would come out.

VIII

He was convinced, a kindred creature
would be allied to him by fate;
that, meanwhile, pinched and glum of feature,
from day to day she could but wait;
and he believed his friends were ready
to put on chains for him, and steady
their hand to grapple slander's cup,
in his defence, and smash it up;
[that there existed, for the indulgence
of human friendship, holy men,
immortals picked by fate for when,
with irresistible refulgence,
their breed would (some years after this)
shine out and bring the world to bliss.]

IX

Compassion, yes, and indignation,
honest devotion to the good,
bitter-sweet glory's inspiration,
already stirred him as they should.
He roamed the world, his lyre behind him;
Schiller and Goethe had refined him,
and theirs was the poetic flame
that fired his soul, to burn the same;
the Muses' lofty arts and fashions,
fortunate one, he'd not disgrace;
but in his songs kept pride of place
for the sublime, and for the passions
of virgin fancy, and again
the charm of what was grave and plain.

X

He sang of love, to love subjected,
his song was limpid in its tune
as infant sleep, or the unaffected
thoughts of a girl, or as the moon
through heaven's expanse serenely flying,
that queen of secrets and of sighing.
He sang of grief and parting-time,
of something vague, some misty clime;
roses romantically blowing;
of many distant lands he sang
where in the heart of silence rang
his sobs, where his live tears were flowing;
he sang of lifetime's yellowed page –
when not quite eighteen years of age.

XI

But in that desert his attainments
only to Eugene showed their worth;
Lensky disliked the entertainments
of neighbouring owners of the earth –
he fled from their resounding chatter!
Their talk, so sound on every matter,
on liquor, and on hay brought in,
on kennels, and on kith and kin,
it had no sparkle of sensation,
it lacked, of course, poetic heart,
sharpness of wit, and social art,
and logic; yet the conversation
upon the side of the distaff –
that was less clever still by half.

XII

Vladimir, wealthy and good-looking,
was asked around as quite a catch –
such is the usual country cooking;
and all the neighbours planned a match
between their girls and this *half-Russian*.
As soon as he appears, discussion
touches obliquely, but with speed,
on the dull life that bachelors lead;
and then it's tea that comes to mention,
and Dunya works the samovar;
and soon they bring her . . . a guitar
and whisper 'Dunya, pay attention!'
then, help me God, she caterwauls:
'Come to me in my golden halls.'

XIII

Lensky of course was quite untainted
by any itch for marriage ties;
instead the chance to get acquainted
with Eugene proved a tempting prize.
So, verse and prose, they came together.
No ice and flame, no stormy weather
and granite, were so far apart.
At first, disparity of heart
rendered them tedious to each other;
then liking grew, then every day
they met on horseback; quickly they
became like brother knit to brother.
Friendship, as I must own to you,
blooms when there's nothing else to do.

XIV

But friendship, as between our heroes,
can't really be: for we've outgrown
old prejudice; all men are zeros,
the units are ourselves alone.
Napoleon's our sole inspiration;
the millions of two-legged creation
for us are instruments and tools;
feeling is quaint, and fit for fools.
More tolerant in his conception
than most, Evgeny, though he knew
and scorned his fellows through and through,
yet, as each rule has its exception,
people there were he glorified,
feelings he valued – from outside.

XV

He smiled as Lensky talked: the heady
perfervid language of the bard,
his mind, in judgement still unsteady,
and always the inspired regard –
to Eugene all was new and thrilling;
he struggled to bite back the chilling
word on his lips, and thought: it's sheer
folly for me to interfere
with such a blissful, brief infection –
even without me it will sink;
but meanwhile let him live, and think
the universe is all perfection;
youth is a fever; we must spare
its natural right to rave and flare.

XVI

Between them, every topic started
reflection or provoked dispute:
treaties of nations long departed,
and good and ill, and learning's fruit,
the prejudices of the ages,
the secrets of the grave, the pages
of fate, and life, each in its turn
became their scrutiny's concern.
In the white heat of some dissension
the abstracted poet would bring forth
fragments of poems from the North,
which, listening with some condescension,
the tolerant Evgeny heard –
but scarcely understood a word.

XVII

But it was passion that preempted
the thoughts of my two anchorites.
From that rough spell at last exempted,
Onegin spoke about its flights
with sighs unconsciously regretful.
Happy is he who's known its fretful
empire, and fled it; happier still
is he who's never felt its will,
he who has cooled down love with parting,
and hate with malice; he whose life
is yawned away with friends and wife
untouched by envy's bitter smarting,
who on a deuce, that famous cheat,
has never staked his family seat.

XVIII

When we've retreated to the banner
of calm and reason, when the flame
of passion's out, and its whole manner
become a joke to us, its game,
its wayward tricks, its violent surging,
its echoes, its belated urging,
reduced to sense, not without pain –
we sometimes like to hear again
passion's rough language talked by others,
and feel once more emotion's ban.
So a disabled soldier-man,
retired, forgotten by his brothers,
in his small shack, will listen well
to tales that young moustachios tell.

XIX

But it's the talent for concealing
that ardent youth entirely lacks;
hate, love, joy, sorrow – every feeling,
it blabs, and spills them in its tracks.
As, lovingly, in his confession,
the poet's heart found full expression,
Eugene, with solemn face, paid heed,
and felt himself love's *invalide*.
Lensky ingenuously related
his conscience's record, and so
Onegin swiftly came to know
his tale of youthful love, narrated
with deep emotion through and through,
to us, though, not exactly new.

XX

Ah, he had loved a love that never
is known today; only a soul
that raves with poetry can ever
be doomed to feel it: there's one goal
perpetually, one goal for dreaming,
one customary object gleaming,
one customary grief each hour!
not separation's chilling power,
no years of absence past returning,
no beauties of a foreign clime,
no noise of gaiety, no time
devoted to the Muse, or learning,
nothing could alter or could tire
this soul that glowed with virgin fire.

XXI

Since earliest boyhood he had doted
on Olga; from heart's ache still spared,
with tenderness he'd watched and noted
her girlhood games; in them he'd shared,
by deep and shady woods protected;
the crown of marriage was projected
for them by fathers who, as friends
and neighbours, followed the same ends.
Away inside that unassuming
homestead, before her parents' gaze,
she blossomed in the graceful ways
of innocence: a lily blooming
in deepest grasses, quite alone,
to bee and butterfly unknown.

XXII

And our young poet – Olga fired him
in his first dream of passion's fruit,
and thoughts of her were what inspired him
to the first moanings of his flute.
Farewell the games of golden childhood!
he fell in love with darkest wildwood,
solitude, stillness and the night,
the stars, the moon – celestial light
to which so oft we've dedicated
those walks amid the gloom and calm
of evening, and those tears, the balm
of secret pain . . . but it's now rated
by judgement of the modern camp
almost as good as a dim lamp.

XXIII

Full of obedience and demureness,
as gay as morning and as clear,
poetic in her simple pureness,
sweet as a lover's kiss, and dear,
in Olga everything expresses –
the skyblue eyes, the flaxen tresses,
smile, voice and movements, little waist –
take any novel, clearly traced
you're sure to find her portrait in it:
a portrait with a charming touch;
once I too liked it very much;
but now it bores me every minute.
Reader, the elder sister now
must be my theme, if you'll allow.

XXIV

Tatyana was her name ... I own it,
self-willed it may be just the same;
but it's the first time you'll have known it,
a novel graced with such a name.
What of it? it's euphonious, pleasant,
and yet inseparably present,
I know it, in the thoughts of all
are old times, and the servants' hall.
We must confess that taste deserts us
even in our names (and how much worse
when we begin to talk of verse);
culture, so far from healing, hurts us;
what it's transported to our shore
is mincing manners – nothing more.

XXV

So she was called Tatyana. Truly
she lacked her sister's beauty, lacked
the rosy bloom that glowed so newly
to catch the eye and to attract.
Shy as a savage, silent, tearful,
wild as a forest deer, and fearful,
Tatyana had a changeling look
in her own home. She never took
to kissing or caressing father
or mother; and in all the play
of children, though as young as they,
she never joined, or skipped, but rather
in silence all day she'd remain
ensconced beside the window-pane.

XXVI

Reflection was her friend and pleasure
right from the cradle of her days;
it touched with reverie her leisure,
adorning all its country ways.
Her tender touch had never fingered
the needle, never had she lingered
to liven with a silk *atour*
the linen stretched on the tambour.
Sign of the urge for domination:
in play with her obedient doll
the child prepares for protocol –
that corps of social legislation –
and to it, with a grave import,
repeats what her mama has taught.

XXVII

Tatyana had no dolls to dandle,
not even in her earliest age;
she'd never tell them news or scandal
or novelties from fashion's page.
Tatyana never knew the attraction
of childish pranks: a chilled reaction
to horror-stories told at night
in winter was her heart's delight.
Whenever *nyanya* had collected
for Olga, on the spreading lawn,
her little friends, Tatyana'd yawn,
she'd never join the game selected,
for she was bored by laughs and noise
and by the sound of silly joys.

XXVIII

She loved the balcony, the session
of waiting for the dawn to blush,
when, in pale sky, the stars' procession
fades from the view, and in the hush
earth's rim grows light, and a forewarning
whisper of breeze announces morning,
and slowly day begins to climb.
In winter, when for longer time
the shades of night within their keeping
hold half the world still unreleased,
and when, by misty moon, the east
is softly, indolently sleeping,
wakened at the same hour of night
Tatyana'd rise by candlelight.

XXIX

From early on she loved romances,
they were her only food . . . and so
she fell in love with all the fancies
of Richardson and of Rousseau.
Her father, kindly, well-regarded,
but in an earlier age retarded,
could see no harm in books; himself
he never took one from the shelf,
thought them a pointless peccadillo;
and cared not what his daughter kept
by way of secret tome that slept
until the dawn beneath her pillow.
His wife, just like Tatyana, had
on Richardson gone raving mad.

XXX

And not because she'd read him, either,
and not because she'd once preferred
Lovelace, or Grandison, or neither;
but in the old days she had heard
about them – nineteen to the dozen –
so often from her Moscow cousin
Princess Alina. She was still
engaged then – but against her will;
loved someone else, not her intended,
someone towards whose heart and mind
her feelings were far more inclined –
this Grandison of hers was splendid,
a fop, a punter on the cards,
and junior Ensign in the Guards.

XXXI

She was like him and always sported
the latest fashions of the town;
but, without asking, they transported
her to the altar and the crown.
The better to dispel her sorrow
her clever husband on the morrow
took her to his estate, where she,
at first, with God knows whom to see,
in tears and violent tossing vented
her grief, and nearly ran away.
Then, plunged in the housekeeper's day,
she grew accustomed, and contented.
In stead of happiness, say I,
custom's bestowed us from on high.

XXXII

For it was custom that consoled her
in grief that nothing else could mend;
soon a great truth came to enfold her
and give her comfort to the end:
she found, in labours and in leisure,
the secret of her husband's measure,
and ruled him like an autocrat –
so all went smoothly after that.
Mushrooms in brine, for winter eating,
fieldwork directed from the path,
accounts, shaved forelocks, Sunday bath;
meantime she'd give the maids a beating
if her cross mood was at its worst –
but *never* asked her husband first.

XXXIII

No, soon she changed her old demeanour:
girls' albums, signed in blood for choice;
Praskovya re-baptized 'Polina';
conversing in a singsong voice;
lacing her stays up very tightly;
pronouncing through her nose politely
the Russian N, like N in French;
soon all that went without a wrench:
album and stays, Princess Alina,
sentiment, notebook, verses, all
she quite forgot – began to call
'Akulka' the onetime Selina,
and introduced, for the last lap,
a quilted chamber-robe and cap.

XXXIV

Her loving spouse with approbation
left her to follow her own line,
trusted her without hesitation,
and wore his dressing-gown to dine.
His life went sailing in calm weather;
sometimes the evening brought together
neighbours and friends in kindly group,
a plain, unceremonious troop,
for grumbling, gossiping and swearing
and for a chuckle or a smile.
The evening passes, and meanwhile
here's tea that Olga's been preparing;
after that, supper's served, and so
bed-time, and time for guests to go.

XXXV

Throughout their life, so calm, so peaceful,
sweet old tradition was preserved:
for them, in Butterweek the greaseful,
Russian pancakes were always served;

⌈

⌉

they needed kvas like air; at table
their guests, for all they ate and drank,
were served in order of their rank.

XXXVI

And so they lived, two ageing mortals,
till he at last was summoned down
into the tomb's wide open portals,
and once again received a crown.
Just before dinner, from his labours
he rested – wept for by his neighbours,
his children and his faithful wife,
far more than most who leave this life.
He was a good and simple *barin*;
above the dust of his remains
the funeral monument explains:
'A humble sinner, Dimitry Larin,
beneath the stone reposes here,
servant of God, and Brigadier.'

XXXVII

Lensky, restored to his manorial
penates, came to cast an eye
over his neighbour's plain memorial,
and offer to that ash a sigh;
sadly he mourned for the departed.
'Poor Yorick,' said he, broken-hearted:
'he dandled me as a small boy.
How many times I made a toy
of his Ochákov decoration!
He destined Olga's hand for me,
kept asking: "shall I live to see" …'
so, full of heart-felt tribulation,
Lensky composed in autograph
a madrigal for epitaph.

XXXVIII

There too, he honoured, hotly weeping,
his parents' patriarchal dust
with lines to mark where they were sleeping . . .
Alas! the generations must,
as fate's mysterious purpose burrows,
reap a brief harvest on their furrows;
they rise and ripen and fall dead:
others will follow where they tread . . .
and thus our race, so fluctuating,
grows, surges, boils, for lack of room
presses its forebears to the tomb.
We too shall find our hour is waiting;
it will be our descendants who
out of this world will crowd us too.

XXIX

So glut yourselves until you're sated
on this unstable life, my friends!
its nullity I've always hated,
I know too surely how it ends.
I'm blind to every apparition;
and yet a distant admonition
of hope sometimes disturbs my heart;
it would be painful to depart
and leave no faint footprint of glory . . .
I never lived or wrote for praise;
yet how I wish that I might raise
to high renown my doleful story,
that there be just one voice which came,
like a true friend, to speak my name.

XL

And someone's heart will feel a quiver,
for maybe fortune will have saved
from drowning's death in Lethe river
the strophe over which I slaved;
perhaps – for flattering hope will linger –
some future dunce will point a finger
at my famed portrait and will say:
he was a poet in his day.
I thank him without reservation,
the peaceful Muses' devotee,
whose memory will preserve for me
the fleeting works of my creation,
whose kindly hand will ruffle down
the laurel in the old man's crown!

CHAPTER THREE

Elle était fille, elle était amoureuse.

MALFILÂTRE

I

'You're off? why, there's a poet for you!'
'Goodbye, Onegin, time I went.'
'Well, I won't hold you up or bore you;
but where are all your evenings spent?'
'At the Larins'!' 'But how mysterious.
For goodness' sake, you can't be serious
killing each evening off like that?'
'You're wrong.' 'But what I wonder at
is this – one sees from here the party:
in first place – listen, am I right? –
a simple Russian family night:
the guests are feasted, good and hearty,
on jam, and speeches in regard
to rains, and flax, and the stockyard.'

II

'I don't see what's so bad about it.'
'Boredom, that's what so bad, my friend.'
'Your modish world, I'll do without it;
give me the homely hearth, and lend . . .'
'You pile one eclogue on another!
for God's sake, that will do. But, brother,
you're really going? Well, I'm sad.
Now, Lensky, would it be so bad
for me to glimpse this Phyllis ever
with whom your thoughts are so obsessed –
pen, tears, and rhymes, and all the rest?
Present me, please.' 'You're joking.' 'Never.'
'Gladly.' 'So when?' 'Why not tonight?
They will receive us with delight.'

III

'Let's go.' The friends, all haste and vigour,
drive there, and with formality
are treated to the fullest rigour
of old-time hospitality.
The protocol is all one wishes:
the jams appear in little dishes;
on a small table's oilcloth sheen
the jug of bilberry wine is seen.

IV

And home was now their destination;
as by the shortest way they flew,
this was our heroes' conversation
secretly overheard by you.
'You yawn, Onegin?' 'As I'm used to.'
'This time I think you've been reduced to
new depths of boredom.' 'No, the same.
The fields are dark, since evening came.
Drive on, Andryushka! quicker, quicker!
the country's pretty stupid here!
oh, *à propos:* Larin's a dear
simple old lady; but the liquor –
I'm much afraid that bilberry wine
won't benefit these guts of mine.

V

'But tell me, which one was Tatyana?'
'She was the one who looked as still
and melancholy as Svetlana,
and sat down by the window-sill.'
'The one you love's the younger daughter?'
'Why not?' 'I'd choose the other quarter
if I, like you, had been a bard.
Olga's no life in her regard:
the roundest face that you've set eyes on,
a pretty girl exactly like
any Madonna by Van Dyck:
a dumb moon, on a dumb horizon.'
Lensky had a curt word to say
and then sat silent all the way.

VI

Meanwhile the news of Eugene coming
to the Larins' had caused a spout
of gossip, and set comment humming
among the neighbours round about.
Conjecture found unending matter:
there was a general furtive chatter,
and jokes and spiteful gossip ran
claiming Tatyana'd found her man;
and some were even testifying
the marriage plans were all exact
but held up by the simple fact
that modish rings were still a-buying.
Of Lensky's fate they said no more –
they'd settled that some years before.

VII

Tatyana listened with vexation
to all this tattle, yet at heart
in indescribable elation,
despite herself, rehearsed the part:
the thought sank in, and penetrated:
she fell in love – the hour was fated . . .
so fires of spring will bring to birth
a seedling fallen in the earth.
Her feelings in their weary session
had long been wasting and enslaved
by pain and languishment; she craved
the fateful diet; by depression
her heart had long been overrun:
her soul was waiting . . . for someone.

VIII

Tatyana now need wait no longer.
Her eyes were opened, and she said
'this is the one!' Ah, ever stronger,
in sultry sleep, in lonely bed,
all day, all night, his presence fills her,
by magic everything instils her
with thoughts of him in ceaseless round.
She hates a friendly voice's sound,
or servants waiting on her pleasure.
Sunk in dejection, she won't hear
the talk of guests when they appear;
she calls down curses on their leisure,
and, when one's least prepared for it,
their tendency to call, and sit.

IX

Now, she devours, with what attention,
delicious novels, laps them up;
and all their ravishing invention
with sheer enchantment fills her cup!
These figures from the world of seeming,
embodied by the power of dreaming,
the lover of Julie Wolmar,
and Malek Adel, de Linar,
and Werther, martyred and doom-laden,
and Grandison beyond compare,
who sets *me* snoring then and there –
all for our tender dreamy maiden
are coloured in a single tone,
all blend into Eugene alone.

X

Seeing herself as a creation –
Clarissa, Julie, or Delphine –
by writers of her admiration,
Tatyana, lonely heroine,
roamed the still forest like a ranger,
sought in her book, that text of danger,
and found her dreams, her secret fire,
the full fruit of her heart's desire;
she sighed, and in a trance coopted
another's joy, another's breast,
whispered by heart a note addressed
to the hero that she'd adopted.
But ours, whatever he might be,
ours was no Grandison – not he.

XI

Lending his tone a grave inflection,
the ardent author of the past
showed one a pattern of perfection
in which his hero's mould was cast.
He gave this figure – loved with passion,
wronged always in disgraceful fashion –
a soul of sympathy and grace,
and brains, and an attractive face.
Always our fervid hero tended
pure passion's flame, and in a trice
would launch into self-sacrifice;
always before the volume ended
due punishment was handed down
to vice, while virtue got its crown.

XII

Today a mental fog enwraps us,
each moral puts us in a doze,
even in novels, vice entraps us,
yes, even there its triumph grows.
Now that the British Muse is able
to wreck a maiden's sleep with fable,
the idol that she'll most admire
is either the *distrait* Vampire,
Melmoth, whose roaming never ceases,
Sbogar, mysterious through and through,
the Corsair, or the Wandering Jew.
Lord Byron, with his shrewd caprices,
dressed up a desperate egoism
to look like sad romanticism.

XIII

In this, dear reader, if you know it,
show me the sense. Divine decree
may wind up my career as poet;
perhaps, though Phoebus warns, I'll see
installed in me a different devil,
and sink to prose's humble level:
a novel on the established line
may then amuse my glad decline.
No secret crimes, and no perditions,
shall make my story grim as hell;
no, quite naively I'll retell
a Russian family's old traditions;
love's melting dreams shall fill my rhyme,
and manners of an earlier time.

XIV

I'll catalogue each simple saying
in father's or old uncle's book,
and tell of children's plighted playing
by ancient limes, or by a brook;
and after jealousy's grim weather
I'll part them, bring them back together;
I'll make them spar another round,
then to the altar, to be crowned.
I'll conjure up that swooning fashion
of ardent speech, that aching flow
of language which, so long ago,
facing a belle I loved with passion,
my tongue kept drawing from the heart –
but now I've rather lost the art.

XV

Tatyana dear, with you I'm weeping:
for you have, at this early date,
into a modish tyrant's keeping
resigned disposal of your fate.
Dear Tanya, you're condemned to perish;
but first, the dreams that hope can cherish
evoke for you a sombre bliss;
you learn life's sweetness, and with this
you drink the magic draught of yearning,
that poison brew; and in your mind
reverie hounds you, and you find
shelter for trysts at every turning;
in front of you, on every hand,
you see your fated tempter stand.

XVI

Tatyana, hunted by love's anguish,
has made the park her brooding-place,
suddenly lowering eyes that languish,
too faint to stir a further pace:
her bosom heaves, her cheeks are staring
scarlet with passion's instant flaring,
upon her lips the breathing dies,
noise in her ears, glare in her eyes . . .
then night comes on; the moon's patrolling
far-distant heaven's vaulted room;
a nightingale, in forest gloom,
sets a sonorous cadence rolling –
Tatyana, sleepless in the dark,
makes to her nurse low-voiced remark:

XVII

'I can't sleep, *nyanya:* it's so stifling!
open the window, sit down near.'
'Why, Tanya, what . . . ?' 'All's dull and trifling.
The olden days, I want to hear . . .'
'What of them, Tanya? I was able,
years back, to call up many a fable;
I kept in mind an ancient store
of tales of girls, and ghosts, and lore:
but now my brain is darkened, Tanya:
now I've forgotten all I knew.
A sorry state of things, it's true!
My mind is fuddled.' 'Tell me, *nyanya,*
your early life, unlock your tongue:
were you in love when you were young?'

XVIII

'What nonsense, Tanya! in those other
ages we'd never heard of love:
why, at the thought, my husband's mother
had chased me to the world above.'
'How did you come to marry, *nyanya*?'
'I reckon, by God's will. My Vanya
was younger still, but at that stage
I was just thirteen years of age.
Two weeks the matchmaker was plying
to see my kin, and in the end
my father blessed me. So I'd spend
my hours in fear and bitter crying.
Then, crying, they untwined my plait,
and sang me to the altar-mat.

XIX

'So to strange kinsfolk I was taken . . .
but you're not paying any heed.'
'Oh nurse, I'm sad, I'm sad, I'm shaken,
I'm sick, my dear, I'm sick indeed.
I'm near to sobbing, near to weeping! . . .'
'You're ill, God have you in his keeping,
the Lord have mercy on us all!
whatever you may need, just call . . .
I'll sprinkle you with holy water,
you're all in fever . . . heavens above.'
'Nurse, I'm not ill; I . . . I'm in love.'
'The Lord God be with you, my daughter!'
and, hands a-tremble, *Nyanya* prayed
and put a cross-sign on the maid.

XX

'I am in love,' Tatyana's wailing
whisper repeated to the crone.
'My dearest heart, you're sick and ailing.'
'I am in love; leave me alone.'
And all the while the moon was shining
and with its feeble glow outlining
the girl's pale charms, her loosened hair,
her drops of tears, and seated there,
in quilted coat, where rays were gleaming
on a small bench by Tanya's bed,
the grey-haired nurse with kerchiefed head;
and everything around was dreaming,
in the deep stillness of the night,
bathed in the moon's inspiring light.

XXI

Tatyana watched the moon, and floated
through distant regions of the heart ...
A thought was born, and quickly noted ...
'Go, nurse, and leave me here apart.
Give me a pen and give me paper,
bring up a table, and a taper;
good night; I swear I'll lie down soon.'
She was alone, lit by the moon.
Elbow on table, spirit seething,
still filled with Eugene, Tanya wrote,
and in her unconsidered note
all a pure maiden's love was breathing.
She folds the page, lays down the plume ...
Tatyana! it's addressed ... to whom?

XXII

I've known too many a haughty beauty,
cold, pure as ice, and as unkind,
inexorably wed to duty,
unfathomable to the mind;
shocked by their modish pride, and fleeing
the utter virtue of their being,
I've run a mile, I must avow,
having deciphered on their brow
hell's terrifying imprecation:
'Abandon hope for evermore.'
Our love is what they most abhor;
our terror is their consolation.
Ladies of such a cast, I think,
you too have seen on Neva's brink.

XXIII

Thronged by adorers, I've detected
another, freakish one, who stays
quite self-absorbed and unaffected
by sighs of passion or by praise.
To my astonishment I've seen her,
having by her severe demeanour
frightened to death a timid love,
revive it with another shove –
at least by a regretful kindness;
at least her tone is sometimes found
more tender than it used to sound.
I've seen how, trustful in his blindness,
the youthful lover once again
runs after what is sweet, and vain.

XXIV

Why is Tatyana guiltier-seeming?
is it that she, poor simple sweet,
believes in her elected dreaming
and has no knowledge of deceit?
that, artless, and without concealing,
her love obeys the laws of feeling,
that she's so trustful, and imbued
by heaven with such an unsubdued
imagination, with such reason,
such stubborn brain, and vivid will,
and heart so tender, it can still
burst to a fiery blaze in season?
Such feckless passion – as I live,
is this then what you can't forgive?

XXV

The flirt has reason's cool volition;
Tatyana's love is no by-play,
she yields to it without condition
like a sweet child. She'll never say:
'By virtue of procrastinating
we'll keep love's price appreciating,
we'll draw it deeper in our net;
first, we'll take vanity, and let
hope sting it, then we'll try deploying
doubts, to exhaust the heart, then fire
jealousy's flame, to light desire;
else, having found his pleasure cloying,
the cunning prisoner can quite well
at any hour escape his cell.'

XXVI

I see another problem looming:
to save the honour of our land
I *must* translate – there's no presuming –
the letter from Tatyana's hand:
her Russian was as thin as vapour,
she never read a Russian paper,
our native speech had never sprung
unhesitating from her tongue,
she wrote in French . . . what a confession!
what can one do? as said above,
until this day, a lady's love
in Russian never found expression,
till now our language – proud, God knows –
has hardly mastered postal prose.

XXVII

They should be forced to read in Russian,
I hear you say. But can you see
a lady – what a grim discussion! –
with *The Well-Meaner* on her knee?
I ask you, each and every poet!
the darling objects – don't you know it? –
for whom, to expiate your crimes,
you've made so many secret rhymes,
to whom your hearts are dedicated,
is it not true that Russian speech,
so sketchily possessed by each,
by all is sweetly mutilated,
and it's the foreign phrase that trips
like native idiom from their lips?

XXVIII

Protect me from such apparition
on dance-floor, at breakup of ball,
as bonneted Academician
or seminarist in yellow shawl!
To me, unsmiling lips bring terror,
however scarlet; free from error
of grammar, Russian language too.
Now, to my cost it may be true
that generations of new beauties,
heeding the press, will make us look
more closely at the grammar-book;
that verse will turn to useful duties;
on me, all this has no effect:
tradition still keeps my respect.

XXIX

No, incorrect and careless chatter,
words mispronounced, thoughts ill-expressed
evoke emotion's pitter-patter,
now as before, inside my breast;
too weak to change, I'm staying vicious,
I still find Gallicism delicious
as youthful sinning, or the strains
of Bogdanóvich's refrains.
But that's enough. My beauty's letter
must now employ my pen; somehow
I gave my word, alas, though now
a blank default would suit me better.
I own it: tender Parny's rhyme
is out of fashion in our time.

XXX

Bard of *The Feasts*, and heart's depression,
if you'd still been with me, dear friend,
I would have had the indiscretion
to ask of you that you transcend
in music's own bewitching fashion
the foreign words a maiden's passion
found for its utterance that night.
Where are you? come – and my own right
with an obeisance I'll hand over . . .
But he, by sad and rocky ways,
with heart that's grown unused to praise,
on Finland's coast a lonely rover –
he doesn't hear when I address
his soul with murmurs of distress.

XXXI

Tatyana's letter, treasured ever
as sacred, lies before me still.
I read with secret pain, and never
can read enough to get my fill.
Who taught her an address so tender,
such careless language of surrender?
Who taught her all this mad, slapdash,
heartfelt, imploring, touching trash
fraught with enticement and disaster?
It baffles me. But I'll repeat
here a weak version, incomplete,
pale transcript of a vivid master,
or *Freischütz* as it might be played
by nervous hands of a schoolmaid:

TATYANA'S LETTER TO ONEGIN

'I write to you — no more confession
is needed, nothing's left to tell.
I know it's now in your discretion
with scorn to make my world a hell.

'But, if you've kept some faint impression
of pity for my wretched state,
you'll never leave me to my fate.
At first I thought it out of season
to speak; believe me: of my shame
you'd not so much as know the name,
if I'd possessed the slightest reason
to hope that even once a week
I might have seen you, heard you speak
on visits to us, and in greeting
I might have said a word, and then
thought, day and night, and thought again
about one thing, till our next meeting.
But you're not sociable, they say:
you find the country godforsaken;
though we ... don't shine in any way,
our joy in you is warmly taken.

'Why did you visit us, but why?
Lost in our backwoods habitation
I'd not have known you, therefore I
would have been spared this laceration.
In time, who knows, the agitation
of inexperience would have passed,

I would have found a friend, another,
and in the role of virtuous mother
and faithful wife I'd have been cast.

'Another! ... No, another never
in all the world could take my heart!
Decreed in highest court for ever ...
heaven's will — for you I'm set apart;
and my whole life has been directed
and pledged to you, and firmly planned;
I know, Godsent one, I'm protected
until the grave by your strong hand:
you'd made appearance in my dreaming;
unseen, already you were dear,
my soul had heard your voice ring clear,
stirred at your gaze, so strange, so gleaming,
long, long ago ... no, that could be
no dream. You'd scarce arrived, I reckoned
to know you, swooned, and in a second
all in a blaze, I said: it's he!

'You know, it's true, how I attended,
drank in your words when all was still —
helping the poor, or while I mended
with balm of prayer my torn and rended
spirit that anguish had made ill.
At this midnight of my condition,
was it not you, dear apparition,
who in the dark came flashing through
and, on my bed-head gently leaning,
with love and comfort in your meaning,

spoke words of hope? But who are you:
the guardian angel of tradition,
or some vile agent of perdition
sent to seduce? Resolve my doubt.
Oh, this could all be false and vain,
a sham that trustful souls work out;
fate could be something else again . . .

'So let it be! for you to keep
I trust my fate to your direction,
henceforth in front of you I weep,
I weep, and pray for your protection . . .
Imagine it: quite on my own
I've no one here who comprehends me,
and now a swooning mind attends me,
dumb I must perish, and alone.
My heart awaits you: you can turn it
to life and hope with just a glance –
or else disturb my mournful trance
with censure – I've done all to earn it!

'I close. I dread to read this page . . .
for shame and fear my wits are sliding . . .
and yet your honour is my gage,
and in it boldly I'm confiding' . . .

XXXII

Now Tanya's groaning, now she's sighing;
the letter trembles in her grip;
the rosy sealing-wafer's drying
upon her feverish tongue; the slip
from off her charming shoulder's drooping,
and sideways her poor head is stooping.
But now the radiance of the moon
is dimmed. Down there the valley soon
comes clearer through the mists of dawning.
Down there, by slow degrees, the stream
has taken on a silvery gleam;
the herdsman's horn proclaimed the morning
and roused the village long ago:
to Tanya, all's an empty show.

XXXIII

She's paid the sunrise no attention,
she sits with head sunk on her breast,
over the note holds in suspension
her seal with its engraven crest.
Softly the door is opened, enter
grey Filatevna, to present her
with a small tray and a teacup.
'Get up, my child, it's time, get up!
Why, pretty one, you're up already!
My early bird! you know, last night
you gave me such a shocking fright!
but now, thank God, you're well and steady,
your night of fretting's left no trace!
fresh as a poppy-flower, your face.'

XXXIV

'Oh nurse, a favour, a petition . . .'
'Command me, darling, as you choose.'
'Now don't suppose . . . let no suspicion . . .
but, nurse, you see . . . Oh, don't refuse . . .'
'My sweet, God warrants me your debtor.'
'Then send your grandson with this letter
quickly to O . . . I mean to that . . .
the neighbour . . . you must tell the brat
that not a syllable be uttered
and not a mention of my name . . .'
'Which neighbour, dear? My head became
in these last years all mixed and fluttered.
We've many neighbours round about;
even to count them throws me out.'

XXXV

'How slow you are at guessing, *nyanya!*'
'My sweet, my dearest heart, I'm old,
I'm old, my mind is blunted, Tanya;
times were when I was sharp and bold:
times were, when master's least suggestion . . .'
'Oh *nyanya, nyanya,* I don't question . . .
what have your wits to do with me?
Now here's a letter, as you see,
addressed to Onegin' . . . 'Well, that's easy.
But don't be cross, my darling friend,
you know I'm *hard to comprehend* . . .
Why have you gone all pale and queasy?'
'It's nothing, nurse, nothing, I say . . .
just send your grandson on his way.'

XXXVI

Hours pass; no answer; waiting, waiting.
No word: another day goes by.
She's dressed since dawn, dead pale; debating,
demanding: *when* will he reply?
Olga's adorer comes a-wooing.
'Tell me, what's your companion doing?'
enquired the lady of the hall:
'it seems that he forgot us all.'
Tatyana flushed, and started shaking.
'Today he promised he'd be here,'
so Lensky answered the old dear:
'the mail explains the time he's taking.'
Tatyana lowered her regard
as at a censure that was hard.

XXVII

Day faded; on the table, glowing,
the samovar of evening boiled,
and warmed the Chinese teapot; flowing
beneath it, vapour wreathed and coiled.
Already Olga's hand was gripping
the urn of perfumed tea, and tipping
into the cups its darkling stream –
meanwhile a hallboy handed cream;
before the window taking station,
plunged in reflection's deepest train,
Tatyana breathed on the cold pane,
and in the misted condensation
with charming forefinger she traced
'OE' devotedly inlaced.

Meanwhile with pain her soul was girdled,
and tears were drowning her regard.
A sudden clatter! . . . blood was curdled . . .
Now nearer . . . hooves . . . and in the yard
Evgeny! 'Ah!' Tatyana, fleeting
light as a shadow, shuns a meeting,
through the back porch runs out and flies
down to the garden, and her eyes
daren't look behind her; fairly dashing –
beds, bridges, lawn, she never stops,
the *allée* to the lake, the copse;
breaking the lilac bushes, smashing
parterres, she runs to rivulet's brink,
to gasp, and on a bench to sink.

XXXIX

She dropped . . . 'It's he! Eugene arriving!
Oh God, what did he think!' A dream
of hope is somehow still surviving
in her torn heart – a fickle gleam;
she trembles, and with fever drumming
awaits him – hears nobody coming.
Maidservants on the beds just now
were picking berries from the bough,
singing in chorus as directed
(on orders which of course presume
that thievish mouths cannot consume
their masters' berries undetected
so long as they're employed in song:
such rustic cunning can't be wrong!) –

THE SONG OF THE GIRLS

'Maidens, pretty maidens all,
dear companions, darling friends,
pretty maidens, romp away,
have your fill of revelry!
Strike the ditty up, my sweets,
ditty of our secret world,
and entice a fellow in
to the circle of our dance.
When we draw a fellow in,
when we see him from afar,
darlings, then we'll run away,
cherries then we'll throw at him,
cherries throw and raspberries
and redcurrants throw at him.
Never come and overhear
ditties of our secret world,
never come and like a spy
watch the games we maidens play.'

XL

They sing; unmoved by their sweet-sounding
choruses, Tanya can but wait,
listless, impatient, for the pounding
within her bosom to abate,
and for her cheeks to cease their blushing;
but wildly still her heart is rushing,
and on her cheeks the fever stays,
more and more brightly still they blaze.
So the poor butterfly will quiver
and beat a nacreous wing when caught
by some perverse schoolboy for sport;
and so in winter-fields will shiver
the hare who from afar has seen
a marksman crouching in the green.

XLI

But finally she heaved a yearning
sigh, and stood up, began to pace;
she walked, but just as she was turning
into the *allée*, face to face,
she found Evgeny, eyes a-glitter,
still as a shadow, grim and bitter;
seared as by fire, she stopped. Today
I lack the strength required to say
what came from this unlooked-for meeting;
my friends, I need to pause a spell,
and walk, and breathe, before I tell
a story that still wants completing;
I need to rest from all this rhyme:
I'll end my tale some other time.

CHAPTER FOUR

La morale est dans la nature des choses.

NECKER

(I, II, III, IV, V, VI)

VII

With womankind, the less we love them,
the easier they become to charm,
the tighter we can stretch above them
enticing nets to do them harm.
There was a period when cold-blooded
debauchery was praised, and studied
as love's technique, when it would blare
its own perfection everywhere,
and heartless pleasure was up-graded;
yes, these were our forefathers' ways,
those monkeys of the good old days:
now Lovelace's renown has faded
as scarlet heels have lost their name
and stately periwigs, their fame.

VIII

How dull are acting and evasion,
diversely urging the same plea,
earnestly striving for persuasion
on points that all long since agree –
and always the self-same objection;
how dull to work for the correction
of prejudice that's never been
harboured by maidens of thirteen!
Who's not disgusted by cajoling,
threats, vows, and simulated fears,
by six-page letters, rings and tears,
gossip, and tricks, and the patrolling
of aunts and mothers, and the thrall
of husband's friendship – worst of all!

IX

Evgeny thought in just this fashion.
From his first youth he'd known the force,
the sufferings of tempestuous passion;
its winds had blown him far off course.
Spoilt by the habit of indulgence,
now dazzled by one thing's effulgence,
now disenchanted with the next,
more and more bored by yearning's text,
bored by success' giddy trifle,
he heard in stillness and in din
a deathless murmur from within,
found that in laughter yawns could stifle:
he killed eight years in such a style,
and wasted life's fine flower meanwhile.

X

Though belles had lost his adoration,
he danced attendance with the best;
rebuffed, found instant consolation;
deceived, was overjoyed to rest.
He followed them without illusion,
lost them without regret's contusion,
scarcely recalled their love, their spite;
just like a casual guest who might
devote to whist an evening party,
who'd sit, and at the end of play
would say goodbye and drive away,
go off to sleep quite hale and hearty,
and in the morning wouldn't know
that self-same evening where he'd go.

XI

Yet Tanya's note made its impression
on Eugene, he was deeply stirred:
that virgin dream and its confession
filled him with thoughts that swarmed
    and whirred;
the flower-like pallor of the maiden,
her look, so sweetly sorrow-laden,
all plunged his soul deep in the stream
of a delicious, guiltless dream . . .
and though perhaps old fires were thrusting
and held him briefly in their sway,
Eugene had no wish to betray
a soul so innocent, so trusting.
But to the garden, to the scene
where Tanya now confronts Eugene.

XII

Moments of silence, quite unbroken;
then, stepping nearer, Eugene said:
'You wrote to me, and nothing spoken
can disavow that. I have read
those words where love, without condition,
pours out its guiltless frank admission,
and your sincerity of thought
is dear to me, for it has brought
feeling to what had long been heartless;
but I won't praise you – let me join
and pay my debt in the same coin
with an avowal just as artless;
hear my confession as I stand
I leave the verdict in your hand.

XIII

'Could I be happy circumscribing
my life in a domestic plot;
had fortune blest me by prescribing
husband and father as my lot;
could I accept for just a minute
the homely scene, take pleasure in it –
then I'd have looked for you alone
to be the bride I'd call my own.
Without romance, or false insistence,
I'll say: with past ideals in view
I would have chosen none but you
as helpmeet in my sad existence,
as gage of all things that were good,
and been as happy . . . as I could!

XIV

'But I was simply not intended
for happiness – that alien role.
Should your perfections be expended
in vain on my unworthy soul?
Believe (as conscience is my warrant),
wedlock for us would be abhorrent.
I'd love you, but inside a day,
with custom, love would fade away;
your tears would flow – but your emotion,
your grief would fail to touch my heart,
they'd just enrage it with their dart.
What sort of roses, in your notion,
would Hymen bring us – blooms that might
last many a day, and many a night!

XV

'What in the world is more distressing
than households where the wife must moan
the unworthy husband through depressing
daytimes and evenings passed alone?
and where the husband, recognizing
her worth (but anathematising
his destiny) without a smile
bursts with cold envy and with bile?
For such am I. When you were speaking
to me so simply, with the fires
and force that purity inspires,
is *this* the man that you were seeking?
can it be true you must await
from cruel fortune such a fate?

XVI

'I've dreams and years past resurrection;
a soul that nothing can renew . . .
I feel a brotherly affection,
or something tenderer still, for you.
Listen to me without resentment:
girls often change to their contentment
light dreams for new ones . . . so we see
each springtime, on the growing tree,
fresh leaves . . . for such is heaven's mandate.
You'll love again, but you must teach
your heart some self-restraint; for each
and every man won't understand it
as I have . . . learn from my belief
that inexperience leads to grief.'

XVII

So went his sermon. Almost dying,
blinded to everything about
by mist of tears, without replying
Tatyana heard Evgeny out.
He gave his arm. In sad abstraction,
by what's called *machinal* reaction,
without a word Tatyana leant
upon it, and with head down-bent
walked homeward round the kitchen garden;
together they arrived, and none
dreamt of reproving what they'd done:
by country freedom, rightful pardon
and happy licence are allowed,
as much as in Moscow the proud.

XVIII

Agree, the way Eugene proceeded
with our poor girl was kind and good;
not for the first time he succeeded
in manifesting, as he could,
a truly noble disposition;
yet people's malice and suspicion
persisted and made no amends.
By enemies, no less by friends
(it's all the same – you well correct us),
he found all kinds of brickbat hurled.
We each have enemies in this world,
but from our friends, good Lord protect us!
Those friends, those friends! it is, I fear,
with cause that I've recalled them here.

XIX

What of it? Nothing. I'm just sending
to sleep some black and empty dreams;
but, inside brackets, I'm contending
there's no ignoble tale that seems
cooked-up where garret-vermin babble,
endorsed by fashionable rabble,
there's no absurdity as such,
no vulgar epigram too much,
which smilingly your friend, supported
by decent company, has not,
without a trace of spite or plot,
a hundred times afresh distorted;
yet he'd back you through thick and thin:
he loves you . . . like your kith and kin!

XX

Hm, hm. Distinguished reader, tell me
how are your *kith and kin* today?
And here my sentiments impel me
for your enlightenment to say
how I interpret this expression:
our kin are folk whom by profession
we have to cherish and admire
with all our hearts, and who require
that in the usual Christmas scrimmage
we visit them, or without fail
send them good wishes through the mail
to ensure that till next time our image
won't even cross their minds by stealth . . .
God grant them years and years of health!

XXI

Of course, the love of tender beauties,
surer than friendship or than kin,
will loyally discharge its duties,
in midst of trouble, storm or din.
Of course. Yet fashion's wild rotation,
yet a capricious inclination,
yet floods of talk around the town . . .
the darling sex is light as down.
Then verdicts from her husband's quarter
are bound, by every virtuous wife,
to be respected all through life:
and so your faithfullest supporter
will disappear as fast as smoke:
for Satan, love's a splendid joke.

XXII

Whom then to credit? *Whom* to treasure?
On whom alone can we depend?
Who is there who will truly measure
his acts and words to suit our end?
Who'll sow no calumnies around us?
Whose fond attentions will astound us?
Who'll never fault our vices, or
whom shall we never find a bore?
Don't let a ghost be your bear-leader,
don't waste your efforts on the air.
Just let *yourself* be your whole care,
your loved one, honourable reader!
Deserving object: there can be
nothing more lovable than he.

XXIII

Then what resulted from the meeting?
Alas, it's not so hard to guess!
Love's frantic torments went on beating
and racking with their strain and stress
that youthful soul, which pined for sadness;
no, all devoured by passion's madness
poor Tanya more intensely burns;
sleep runs from her, she turns and turns . . .
and health, life's sweetness and its shimmer,
smiles, and a maiden's tranquil poise,
have vanished, like an empty noise,
while dear Tatyana's youth grows dimmer:
so a storm-shadow wraps away
in dark attire the new-born day.

XXIV

Poor Tanya's bloom begins to languish,
and pale, and fade without a word!
there's nothing can employ her anguish,
no sound by which her soul is stirred.
Neighbours in whispered tones are taking
council, and with profound head-shaking
conclude that it's high time she wed! . . .
But that's enough. At once, in stead,
I'll gladden your imagination,
reader, by painting you a scene
of happy love. For I have been
too long, against my inclination,
held in constraint by pity's touch:
I love my Tatyana too much!

XXV

From hour to hour a surer capture
for Olga's beauty, Lensky gives
his soul to a delicious rapture
that fills him and in which he lives.
He's always with her: either seated
in darkness in her room, or treated
to garden walks, as arm in arm
they while away the morning's calm.
What else? Quite drunk with love's illusion,
he even dares, once in a while,
emboldened by his Olga's smile,
and plunged in tender shame's confusion,
to play with a dishevelled tress,
or kiss the border of her dress.

XXVI

He reads to Olga on occasion,
for her improvement, a *roman*,
of moralistical persuasion,
more searching than Chateaubriand;
but in it there are certain pages
(vain twaddle, fables of the ages,
talk that might turn a young girl's head)
which with a blush he leaves unread.
As far removed as they were able
from all the world, they sat and pored
in deepest thought at the chess-board
for hours, with elbows on the table –
then Lensky moved his pawn, and took,
deep in distraction, his own rook.

XXVII

Even at home his occupation
is only Olga: he relieves
with careful schemes of decoration
an album's loose and floating sheaves.
Sometimes a landscape's represented,
a tomb, a Cyprian shrine's invented,
a lyre, and on it perched, a dove –
in ink with colour-wash above;
then on the leaves of recollection,
below the others who have signed
he leaves a tender verse behind,
a dream's mute monument, reflection
of instant thoughts, a fleeting trace
still after many years in place.

XXVIII

Often of course you'll have inspected
the album of a country miss
where scribbling friends have interjected
frontwise and back, that way and this.
With spelling scrambled to perdition,
the unmetric verses of tradition
are entered here, in friendship's gage,
shortened, or lengthened off the page.
On the first sheet you'll find a question:
'Qu'écrirez-vous sur ces tablettes?'
and, under, 'toute à vous Annette';
then, on the last page, the suggestion:
'who loves you more than I, let's see
him prove it, writing after me.'

XXIX

There you're entirely sure of finding
two hearts, a torch, and a nosegay;
and there, love's protestations, binding
until the tombstone; there one day
some regimental bard has added
a stanza villainously padded.
In such an album, friends, I too
am always glad to write, it's true,
convinced at heart that my most zealous
nonsense will earn indulgent looks,
nor will my scribbling in such books
attract the sneering of the jealous,
or make men seriously discuss
if I show wit in jesting thus.

XXX

But you, grand tomes I loathe with passion,
odd volumes from the devil's shelf,
in which the rhymester-man-of-fashion
is forced to crucify himself,
portfolios nobly illustrated
with Tolstoy's brush, or decorated
by Baratynsky's wondrous pen,
God's thunder burn you up! And when
some splendid lady is referring
to me her best in-quarto tome,
the fear and rage with which I foam!
Deep down, an epigram is stirring
that I'm just longing to indite –
but madrigals I've got to write!

XXXI

No madrigals were for inscribing
by Lensky in his Olga's book;
his style breathed love, and not the gibing
coldness of wit; each note he took,
each news of her he'd been imbibing –
all was material for transcribing:
with lively and pellucid look,
his elegies flow like a brook.
So you, inspired Yazykov, sobbing
with bursts of passion from the heart,
sing God knows whom, compose with art
a suite of elegies that, throbbing,
sooner or later will relate
the entire story of your fate.

XXXII

But soft! You hear? A scowling critic,
bidding us to reject for good
the elegy, grown paralytic,
commands our rhymester-brotherhood:
'oh, quit your stale, your tedious quacking,
and your alas-ing and alack-ing
about what's buried in the past:
sing about something else at last!'
All right, you want the resurrection
of trumpet, dagger, mask and sword,
and dead ideas from that old hoard,
all brought to life at your direction.
Not so? 'No, sirs, the ode's the thing,
that's the refrain that you should sing,

XXXIII

'as sung of old, in years of glory,
as instituted long ago.'
Only the ode, that solemn story!
Enough, my friends; it's all so-so.
Remember the retort satiric!
Is *Others' View*, that clever lyric,
really more bearable to you
than what our sorrowing rhymesters do?
'The elegy's just vain protesting,
empty the purpose it proclaims,
while odes have high and noble aims ...'
That point I wouldn't mind contesting,
but hold my tongue, lest it appears
I'll set two ages by the ears.

XXXIV

In love with fame, by freedom smitten,
with storm and tumult in his head,
what odes Vladimir might have written –
but Olga would have never read!
Bards of our tearful generation,
have you read lines of your creation
to your loved ones? They do maintain
that this of all things for a swain
is the supreme reward. Precisely,
blest the poor lover who reads out
his dreams, while she whom they're about,
that languid beauty, listens nicely –
blest … though perhaps her fancy's caught
in fact by some quite different thought.

XXXV

But I myself read my bedizened
fancies, my rhythmic search for truth,
to nobody except a wizened
nanny, companion of my youth;
or, after some dull dinner's labour,
I buttonhole a wandering neighbour
and in a corner make him choke
on tragedy; but it's no joke,
when, utterly worn out by rhyming,
exhausted and done up, I take
a rambling walk beside my lake,
and duck get up; with instant timing,
alarmed by my melodious lay,
they leave their shores and fly away.

XXXVI

⌜My gaze pursues them . . . but on station
the hunter in the wood will swear
at verse, and hiss an imprecation,
and ease his catch with all due care.
We each enjoy a special hobby,
each of us has his favourite lobby:
one sees a duck and aims his gun,
one raves in verse like me, and one
hunts cheeky flies, with swatter sweeping,
one leads the multitude in thought,
one finds in war amusing sport,
one wallows in delicious weeping;
the wine-addict adores the cup:
and good and bad are all mixed up.⌟

XXXVII

But what about Eugene? With reason
reader, you ask, and I'll expound –
craving your tolerance in season –
the programme of his daily round.
In summertime – for he was leading
a hermit's life – he'd be proceeding
on foot, by seven o'clock, until
he reached the stream below the hill;
lightly attired, like the creator
of Gulnare, he would play a card
out of the hand of that same bard:
he'd swim this Hellespont; then later
he'd drink his coffee, flutter through
the pages of some dull review,
then dress . . .

(XXXVIII) XXXIX

Books, riding, walks, sleep heavy-laden,
the shady wood, the talking stream;
sometimes from a fair, black-eyed maiden
the kiss where youth and freshness gleam;
a steed responsive to the bridle,
and dinner with a touch of idle
fancy, a wine serene in mood,
tranquillity, and solitude –
Onegin's life, you see, was holy;
unconsciously he let it mount
its grip on him, forgot to count
bright summer days that passed so slowly,
forgot to think of town and friends
and tedious means to festive ends.

XL

Our evanescent northern summer
parodies winter in the south;
it's like a vanishing newcomer –
but here we must control our mouth.
The sky breathed autumn, time was flowing,
and good old sun more seldom glowing;
the days grew shorter, in the glade
with mournful sound the secret shade
was stripped away, and mists encroaching
lay on the fields; in caravan
the clamorous honking geese began
their southward flight: one saw approaching
the season which is such a bore –
November stood outside the door.

XLI

Dawn comes in mist and chill; no longer
do fields echo with work and shout;
in pairs, their hunger driving stronger,
on the highroad the wolves come out;
the horse gets wind of them and, snorting,
sets the wise traveller cavorting
up the hillside at breakneck pace;
no longer does the herdsman chase
his beasts outdoors at dawn, nor ringing
at noontime does his horn resound
as it assembles them around;
while in the hut a girl is singing;
she spins and, friend of winter nights,
the matchwood chatters as it lights.

XLII

Hoar-frost that crackles with a will is
already silvering all the plain . . .
(the reader thinks the rhyme is *lilies:*
here, seize it quick for this quatrain!)
Like modish parquetry, the river
glitters beneath its icing-sliver;
boy-tribes with skates on loudly slice
their joyous way across the ice;
a red-foot goose, weight something fearful,
anticipates a swim, in stead
tries out the ice with cautious tread,
and skids and tumbles down; the cheerful
first flakes of snow whirl round and sink
in stars upon the river-brink.

XLIII

In backwoods, how d'you pass this season?
Walking? The country that you roam
is a compulsive bore by reason
of its unvarnished monochrome.
Riding on the lugubrious prairie?
Your horse, blunt-shoed and all unwary,
will find the ice elude his grip
and, any moment, down he'll slip.
Or, in your lonely homestead, moping,
you'll read: here's Pradt, here's Walter Scott!
to pass the evening. No? then tot
up your accounts, and raging, toping,
let evening pass, tomorrow too –
in triumph you'll see winter through!

XLIV

Childe-Harold-like, Eugene's devoting
his hours to dreaming them away:
he wakes; a bath where ice is floating;
and then, indoors the livelong day,
alone, and sunk in calculation,
with a blunt cue for the duration,
from early morning on he will
at two-ball billiards prove his skill;
then, country evening fast arriving,
billiards are dropped, cue put to bed;
before the fire a table's spread;
Evgeny waits: and here comes driving,
with three roan horses in a line
Vladimir Lensky. Quick, let's dine!

XLV

From widow Clicquot and from Moët,
the draught whose blessings are agreed,
in frosted bottle, for the poet
is brought to table at full speed.
Bubbles like Hippocrene are spraying;
once, with its foaming and its playing,
(a simile of this and that)
it held me captive; tit for tat,
friends, recollect how I surrendered
my last poor lepton for a sup!
recall, by its bewitching cup,
how many follies were engendered;
how many lines of verse, and themes
for jokes, and rows, and merry dreams!

XLVI

Yet hissing froth deals a malicious,
perfidious blow to my inside,
and now it's Bordeaux the judicious
that I prefer to Champagne's tide;
to Aÿ's vintage in the sequel
I find myself no longer equal;
for, mistress-like, it's brilliant, vain,
lively, capricious, and inane . . .
But in misfortune or displeasure,
Bordeaux, you're like a faithful friend,
a true companion to the end,
ready to share our quiet leisure
with your good offices, and so
long life to our dear friend, Bordeaux!

XLVII

The fire was dying; cinders faintly
covered the golden coal – the steam
tumbled and whirled and twisted quaintly
its barely noticeable stream.
The hearth was low beyond all stoking.
Straight up the chimney, pipes were smoking.
Still on the board, the beakers hissed,
and evening now drew on in mist ...
(I like a friendly conversation,
the enjoyment of a friendly drink,
at hours, which, why I cannot think,
somehow have got the designation
of *time between the wolf and dog*.)
Now hear the friends in dialogue:

XLVIII

'Tell me, our neighbours, are they thriving?
and how's Tatyana? Olga too,
your dashing one, is she surviving?'
'Just half a glass more ... that will do ...
All flourishing; they send their duty.
Take Olga's shoulders now – the beauty!
What breasts! What soul! ... We'll go one day
visit the family, what d'you say?
if you come with me, they'll be flattered;
or else, my friend, how does it look?
you called there twice, and since then took
no notice of them. But I've chattered
so much, I'm left no time to speak!
of course! you're bidden there next week.'

XLIX

'I?' 'Saturday. The invitation
Olinka and her mother sent:
Tatyana's name day celebration.
It's right and proper that you went.'
'But there'll be such a rout and scrabble
with every different kind of rabble ...'
'No, no, I'm sure the party's small.
Relations. No one else at all.
Let's go, our friendship's worth the labour!'
'All right, I'll come then ...' 'What a friend!'
He drained his glass down to the end
by way of toast to their fair neighbour;
then he began to talk once more
of Olga: love's that kind of bore!

L

Lensky rejoiced. His designated
rapture was just two weeks ahead;
love's crown, delectable, awaited
his transports, and the marriage-bed
in all its mystery. Hymen's teasing,
the pain, the grief, the marrow-freezing
onset of the incipient yawn,
were from his vision quite withdrawn.
While under the connubial banner
I can see naught, as Hymen's foe,
beyond a string of dull tableaux,
a novel in Lafontaine's manner ...
my wretched Lensky in his heart
was just created for the part.

LI

And he was loved ... at least he never
doubted of it, so lived in bliss.
Happy a hundredfold, whoever
can lean on faith, who can dismiss
cold reason, sleep in sensual welter
like a drunk traveller in a shelter,
or, sweeter, like a butterfly
in flowers of spring it's drinking dry;
but piteous he, the all-foreseeing,
the sober head, detesting each
human reaction, every speech
in the expression of its being,
whose heart experience has cooled
and saved from being charmed or fooled!

CHAPTER FIVE

O, never know these frightful dreams,
thou, my Svetlana!

ZHUKOVSKY

I

That year the season was belated
and autumn lingered, long and slow;
expecting winter, nature waited –
only in January the snow,
night of the second, started flaking.
Next day Tatyana, early waking,
saw through the window, morning-bright,
roofs, flowerbeds, fences, all in white,
panes patterned by the finest printer,
with trees decked in their silvery kit,
and jolly magpies on the flit,
and hills that delicately winter
had with its brilliant mantle crowned –
and glittering whiteness all around.

II

Winter! . . . The countryman, enchanted,
breaks a new passage with his sleigh;
his nag has smelt the snow, and planted
a shambling hoof along the way;
a saucy kibítka is slicing
its furrow through the powdery icing;
the driver sits and cuts a dash
in sheepskin coat with scarlet sash.
Here comes the yard-boy, who has chosen
his pup to grace the sledge, while he
becomes a horse for all to see;
the rogue has got a finger frozen:
it hurts, he laughs, and all in vain
his mother taps the window-pane.

III

But you perhaps find no attraction
in any picture of this kind:
for nature's unadorned reaction
has something low and unrefined.
Fired by the god of inspiration,
another bard in exaltation
has painted for us the first snow
with each nuance of wintry glow:
he'll charm you with his fine invention,
he'll take you prisoner, you'll admire
secret sledge-rides in verse of fire;
but I've not got the least intention
just now of wrestling with his shade,
nor his, who sings of Finland's maid.

IV

Tanya (profoundly Russian being,
herself not knowing how or why)
in Russian winters thrilled at seeing
the cold perfection of the sky,
hoar-frost and sun in freezing weather,
sledges, and tardy dawns together
with the pink glow the snows assume
and festal evenings in the gloom.
The Larins kept the old tradition:
maid-servants from the whole estate
would on those evenings guess the fate
of the two girls; their premonition
pointed each year, for time to come,
at soldier-husbands, and the drum.

V

Tatyana shared with full conviction
the simple faith of olden days
in dreams and cards and their prediction,
and portents of the lunar phase.
Omens dismayed her with their presage;
each object held a secret message
for her instruction, and her breast
was by forebodings much oppressed.
The tomcat, mannered and affected,
that sat above the stove and purred
and washed its face, to her brought word
that visitors must be expected.
If suddenly aloft she spied
the new moon, horned, on her left side,

VI

her face would pale, she'd start to quiver.
In the dark sky, a shooting star
that fell, and then began to shiver,
would fill Tatyana from afar
with perturbation and with worry;
and while the star still flew, she'd hurry
to whisper it her inmost prayer.
And if she happened anywhere
to meet a black monk, or if crossing
her path a hare in headlong flight
ran through the fields, sheer panic fright
would leave her dithering and tossing.
By dire presentiment awestruck,
already she'd assume ill-luck.

VII

Yet – fear itself she found presented
a hidden beauty in the end:
our disposition being invented
by nature, contradiction's friend.
Christmas came on. What joy, what gladness!
Yes, youth divines, in giddy madness,
youth which has nothing to regret,
before which life's horizon yet
lies bright, and vast beyond perceiving;
spectacled age divines as well,
although it's nearly heard the knell,
and all is lost beyond retrieving;
no matter: hope, in child's disguise,
is there to lisp its pack of lies.

VIII

Tatyana looks with pulses racing
at sunken wax inside a bowl:
beyond a doubt, its wondrous tracing
foretells for her some wondrous role;
from dish of water, rings are shifted
in due succession; hers is lifted
and at the very self-same time
the girls sing out the ancient rhyme:
'The peasants there have wealth abounding,
they heap up silver with a spade;
and those we sing for will be paid
in goods and fame!' But the sad-sounding
ditty portends a loss; more dear
is 'Kit' to every maiden's ear.

IX

The sky is clear, the earth is frozen;
the heavenly lights in glorious quire
tread the calm, settled path they've chosen . . .
Tatyana in low-cut attire
goes out into the courtyard spaces
and trains a mirror till it faces
the moon; but in the darkened glass
the only face to shake and pass
is sad old moon's . . . Hark! snow is creaking . . .
a passer-by; and on tiptoe
she flies as fast as she can go;
and 'what's your name?' she asks him, speaking
in a melodious, flute-like tone.
He looks, and answers: 'Agafon.'

X

Prepared for prophecy and fable,
she did what nurse advised she do
and in the bath-house had a table
that night, in secret, set for two;
then sudden fear attacked Tatyana . . .
I too – when I recall Svetlana
I'm terrified – so let it be . . .
Tatyana's rites are not for me.
She's dropped her sash's silken billow;
Tanya's undressed, and lies in bed.
Lel floats about above her head;
and underneath her downy pillow
a young girl's looking-glass is kept.
Now all was still. Tatyana slept.

XI

She dreamt of portents. In her dreaming
she walked across a snowy plain
through gloom and mist; and there came
    streaming
a furious, boiling, heaving main
across the drift-encumbered acres,
a raging torrent, capped with breakers,
a flood on which no frosty band
had been imposed by winter's hand;
two poles that ice had glued like plaster
were placed across the gulf to make
a flimsy bridge whose every quake
spelt hazard, ruin and disaster;
she stopped at the loud torrent's bound,
perplexed . . . and rooted to the ground.

XII

As if before some mournful parting
Tatyana groaned above the tide;
she saw no friendly figure starting
to help her from the other side;
but suddenly a snowdrift rumbled,
and what came out? a hairy, tumbled,
enormous bear; Tatyana yelled,
the bear let out a roar, and held
a sharp-nailed paw towards her; bracing
her nerves, she leant on it her weight,
and with a halting, trembling gait
above the water started tracing
her way; she passed, then as she walked
the bear – what next? – behind her stalked.

XIII

A backward look is fraught with danger;
she speeds her footsteps to a race,
but from her shaggy-liveried ranger
she can't escape at any pace –
the odious bear still grunts and lumbers.
Ahead of them a pinewood slumbers
in the full beauty of its frown;
the branches all are weighted down
with tufts of snow; and through the lifted
summits of aspen, birch and lime,
the nightly luminaries climb.
No path to see: the snow has drifted
across each bush, across each steep,
and all the world is buried deep.

XIV

She's in the wood, the bear still trails her.
There's powdery snow up to her knees;
now a protruding branch assails her
and clasps her neck; and now she sees
her golden earrings off and whipping;
and now the crunchy snow is stripping
her darling foot of its wet shoe,
her handkerchief has fallen too;
no time to pick it up – she's dying
with fright, she hears the approaching bear;
her fingers shake, she doesn't dare
to lift her skirt up; still she's flying,
and he pursuing, till at length
she flies no more, she's lost her strength.

XV

She's fallen in the snow – alertly
the bear has raised her in his paws;
and she, submissively, inertly –
no move she makes, no breath she draws;
he whirls her through the wood . . . a hovel
shows up through trees, all of a grovel
in darkest forest depths and drowned
by dreary snowdrifts piled around;
there's a small window shining in it,
and from within come noise and cheer;
the bear explains: 'my cousin's here –
come in and warm yourself a minute!'
he carries her inside the door
and sets her gently on the floor.

XVI

Tatyana looks, her faintness passes:
bear's gone; a hallway, no mistake;
behind the door the clash of glasses
and shouts suggest a crowded wake;
so, seeing there no rhyme or reason,
no meaning in or out of season,
she peers discreetly through a chink
and sees . . . whatever do you think?
a group of monsters round a table,
a dog with horns, a goatee'd witch,
a rooster head, and on the twitch
a skeleton jerked by a cable,
a dwarf with tail, and a half-strain,
a hybrid cross of cat and crane.

XVII

But ever stranger and more fearful:
a crayfish rides on spider-back;
on goose's neck, a skull looks cheerful
and swaggers in a red calpack;
with bended knees a windmill dances,
its sails go flap-flap as it prances;
song, laughter, whistle, bark and champ,
and human words, and horse's stamp!
But how she jumped, when in this hovel
among the guests she recognized
the man she feared and idolized –
who else? – the hero of our novel!
Onegin sits at table too,
he eyes the door, looks slyly through.

XVIII

He nods – they start to fuss and truckle;
he drinks – all shout and take a swill;
he laughs – they all begin to chuckle;
he scowls – and the whole gang are still;
he's host, that's obvious. Thus enlightened
Tanya's no longer quite so frightened
and, curious now about the lot,
opens the door a tiny slot . . .
but then a sudden breeze surprises,
puts out the lamps; the whole brigade
of house-familiars stands dismayed . . .
with eyes aflame Onegin rises
from table, clattering on the floor;
all stand. He walks towards the door.

XIX

Now she's alarmed; in desperate worry
Tatyana struggles to run out –
she can't; and in her panic hurry
she flails around, she tries to shout –
she can't; Evgeny's pushed the portal,
and to the vision of those mortal
monsters the maiden stood revealed.
Wildly the fearful laughter pealed;
the eyes of all, the hooves, the snozzles,
the bleeding tongues, the tufted tails,
the tusks, the corpse's finger-nails,
the horns, and the moustachio'd nozzles –
all point at her, and all combine
to bellow out: 'she's mine, she's mine.'

XX

'She's *mine!*' Evgeny's voice of thunder
clears in a flash the freezing room;
the whole thieves' kitchen flies asunder,
the girl remains there in the gloom
alone with him; Onegin takes her
into a corner, gently makes her
sit on a flimsy bench, and lays
his head upon her shoulder . . . blaze
of sudden brightness . . . it's too curious . . .
Olga's appeared upon the scene,
and Lensky follows her . . . Eugene,
eyes rolling, arms uplifted, furious,
damns the intruders; Tanya lies
and almost swoons, and almost dies.

XXI

Louder and louder sounds the wrangle:
Eugene has caught up, quick as quick,
a carving-knife – and in the tangle
Lensky's thrown down. The murk is thick
and growing thicker; then, heart-shaking,
a scream rings out . . . the cabin's quaking . . .
Tanya comes to in utter fright . . .
she looks, the room is getting light –
outside, the scarlet rays of dawning
play on the window's frosted lace;
in through the door, at swallow's pace,
pinker than glow of Northern morning,
flits Olga: 'now, tell me straight out,
who was it that you dreamt about?'

XXII

Deaf to her sister's intervention,
Tatyana simply lay in bed,
devoured a book with rapt attention,
and kept quite silent while she read.
The book displayed, not so you'd know it,
no magic fancies of the poet,
no brilliant truth, no vivid scene;
and yet by Vergil or Racine
by Scott, by Seneca, or Byron,
even by *Ladies' Fashion Post*,
no one was ever so engrossed:
Martin Zadéka was the siren,
dean of Chaldea's learned team,
arch-commentator of the dream.

XXIII

This work of the profoundest learning
was brought there by a huckster who
one day came down that lonely turning,
and to Tanya, when he was through,
swapped it for odd tomes of *Malvina*,
but just to make the bargain keener,
he charged three roubles and a half,
and took two *Petriads* in calf,
a grammar, a digest of fable,
and volume three of Marmontel.
Since then Martin Zadéka's spell
bewitches Tanya ... he is able
to comfort her in all her woes,
and every night shares her repose.

XXIV

Tatyana's haunted by her vision,
plagued by her ghastly dream, and tries
to puzzle out with some precision
just what the nightmare signifies.
Searching the table exegetic
she finds, in order alphabetic:
bear, blackness, blizzard, bridge and crow,
fir, forest, hedgehog, raven, snow
etcetera. But her trepidation
Martin Zadéka fails to mend;
the horrid nightmare must portend
a hideous deal of tribulation.
For several days she peaked and pined
in deep anxiety of mind.

XXV

But now Aurora's crimson fingers
from daybreak valleys lift the sun;
the morning light no longer lingers,
the festal name day has begun.
Since dawn, whole families have been driving
towards the Larins' and arriving
in sledded coaches and coupés,
in britzkas, kibítkas and sleighs.
The hall is full of noise and hustle,
in the salon new faces meet,
and kisses smack as young girls greet;
there's yap of pugs, and laughs, and bustle;
the threshold's thronged, wet-nurses call,
guests bow, feet scrape, and children squall.

XXVI

Here with his wife, that bulging charmer,
fat Pústyakov has driven in;
Gvozdín, exemplary farmer,
whose serfs are miserably thin;
and the Skotínins, grizzled sages,
with broods of children of all ages,
from thirty down to two; and stop,
here's Petushkóv, the local fop;
and look, my cousin's come, Buyánov,
in a peaked cap, all dust and fluff, –
you'll recognize him soon enough, –
and counsellor (retired) Flyánov,
that rogue, backbiter, pantaloon,
bribe-taker, glutton and buffoon.

XXVII

Here, in his red peruke and glasses,
late of Tambov, Monsieur Triquet
has come with Kharlikov; he passes
for witty; in his Gallic way
inside a pocket Triquet nurses,
addressed to Tanya, certain verses
set to well-known children's glee:
'réveillez-vous, belle endormie'.
He found them in some old collection,
printed among outmoded airs;
Triquet, ingenious poet, dares
to undertake their resurrection,
and for *belle Nina*, as it read,
he's put *belle Tatiana* instead.

XXVIII

And from the nearby Army station
the Major's here: he's all the rage
with our Mamas, and a sensation
with demoiselles of riper age;
his news has set the party humming!
the regimental band is coming,
sent at the Colonel's own behest.
A ball: the joy of every guest!
Young ladies jump for future blisses . . .
But dinner's served, so two by two
and arm in arm they all go through;
round Tanya congregate the misses,
the men confront them, face to face:
they sit, they cross themselves for grace.

XXIX

They buzz – but then all talk's suspended –
jaws masticate as minutes pass;
the crash of plates and knives is blended
with the resounding chime of glass.
And now there's gradually beginning
among the guests a general dinning:
none listens when the others speak,
all shout and argue, laugh and squeak.
Then doors are opened, Lensky enters,
Onegin too. 'Good Lord, at last!'
the hostess cries and, moving fast,
the guests squeeze closer to the centres;
they shove each plate, and every chair,
and shout, and make room for the pair.

XXX

Just facing Tanya's where they're sitting;
and paler than the moon at dawn,
she lowers darkened eyes, unwitting,
and trembles like a hunted fawn.
From violent passions fast pulsating
she's nearly swooned, she's suffocating;
the friends' salute she never hears
and from her eyes the eager tears
are almost bursting; she's quite ready,
poor girl, to drop into a faint,
but will, and reason's strong constraint,
prevailed, and with composure steady
she sat there; through her teeth a word
came out so soft, it scarce was heard.

XXXI

The nervous-tragical reaction,
girls' tears, their swooning, for Eugene
had long proved tedious to distraction:
he knew too well that sort of scene.
Now, faced with this enormous revel,
he'd got annoyed, the tricky devil.
He saw the sad girl's trembling state,
looked down in an access of hate,
pouted, and swore in furious passion
to wreak, by stirring Lensky's ire,
the best revenge one could desire.
Already, in exultant fashion,
he watched the guests and, as he dined,
caricatured them in his mind.

Tanya's distress had risked detection
not only by Evgeny's eye;
but looks and talk took the direction,
that moment, of a luscious pie
(alas, too salted); now they're bringing
bottles to which some pitch is clinging:
Tsimlyansky wine, between the meat
and the *blancmanger*, then a fleet
of goblets, tall and slender pretties;
how they remind me of your stem,
Zizi, my crystal and my gem,
you object of my guileless ditties!
with draughts from love's enticing flask,
you made me drunk as one could ask!

Freed from its dripping cork, the bottle
explodes; wine fizzes up ... but stay:
solemn, too long compelled to throttle
his itching verse, Monsieur Triquet
is on his feet – in utter stillness
the party waits. Seized with an illness
of swooning, Tanya nearly dies;
and, scroll in hand, before her eyes
Triquet sings, out of tune. Loud clapping
and cheers salute him. Tanya must
thank him by curtseying to the dust;
great bard despite his modest trapping,
he's first to toast her in the bowl,
then he presents her with the scroll.

XXXIV

Compliment and congratulation;
Tanya thanks each one with a phrase.
When Eugene's turn for salutation
arrives, the girl's exhausted gaze,
her discomposure, her confusion,
expose his soul to an intrusion
of pity: in his silent bow,
and in his look there shows somehow
a wondrous tenderness. And whether
it was that he'd been truly stirred,
or half-unwittingly preferred
a joking flirt, or both together,
there was a softness in his glance:
it brought back Tanya from her trance.

XXXV

Chairs are pushed outward, loudly rumbling,
and all into the salon squeeze,
as from their luscious hive go tumbling
fieldward, in noisy swarm, the bees.
The banquet's given no cause for sneezing,
neighbours in high content are wheezing;
ladies at the fireside confer,
in corners whispering girls concur;
now, by green tablecloths awaited,
the eager players are enrolled –
Boston and ombre for the old,
and whist, that's now so keenly fêted –
pursuits of a monotonous breed
begot by boredom out of greed.

XXXVI

By now whist's heroes have completed
eight rubbers; and by now eight times
they've moved around and been reseated;
and tea's brought in. Instead of chimes
I like to tell the time by dinner
and tea and supper; there's an inner
clock in the country rings the hour;
no fuss; our belly has the power
of any Bréguet: and in passing
I'll just remark, my verses talk
as much of banquets and the cork
and eatables beyond all classing
as yours did, Homer, godlike lord,
whom thirty centuries have adored!

⌈XXXVII

At feasts, though, full of pert aggression,
I put your genius to the test,
I make magnanimous confession,
in other things you come off best:
your heroes, raging and ferocious,
your battles, lawless and atrocious,
your Zeus, your Cypris, your whole band
have clearly got the upper hand
of Eugene, cold as all creation,
of plains where boredom reigns complete,
or of Istómina, my sweet,
and all our modish education;
but your vile Helen's not my star –
no, Tanya's more endearing far.

XXXVIII

No one will think that worth gainsaying,
though Menelaus, in Helen's name,
may spend a century in flaying
the hapless Phrygians all the same,
and although Troy's greybeards, collected
around Priam the much-respected,
may chorus, when she comes in sight,
that Menelaus was quite right –
and Paris too. But hear my pleading:
as battles go, I've not begun;
don't judge the race before it's run –
be good enough to go on reading:
there'll be a fight. For that I give
my word; no welshing, as I live.]

XXXIX

Here's tea: the girls have just, as bidden,
taken the saucers in their grip,
when, from behind the doorway, hidden
bassoons and flutes begin to trip.
Elated by the music's blaring,
Petushkóv, local Paris, tearing,
his tea with rum quite left behind,
approaches Olga; Lensky's signed
Tatyana on; Miss Kharlikova,
that nubile maid of riper age,
is seized by Tambov's poet-sage;
Buyánov whirls off Pustyakova;
they all have swarmed into the hall,
and in full brilliance shines the ball.

XL

Right at the outset of my story
(if you'll turn back to chapter one)
I meant to paint, with Alban's glory,
a ball in Petersburg; but fun
and charming reverie's vain deflection
absorbed me in the recollection
of certain ladies' tiny feet.
Enough I've wandered in the suite
of your slim prints! though this be treason
to my young days, it's time I turned
to wiser words and deeds, and learned
to demonstrate some signs of reason:
let no more such digressions lurk
in this fifth chapter of my work.

XLI

And now, monotonously dashing
like mindless youth, the waltz goes by
with spinning noise and senseless flashing
as pair by pair the dancers fly.
Revenge's hour is near, and after
Evgeny, full of inward laughter,
has gone to Olga, swept the girl
past all the assembly in a whirl,
he takes her to a chair, beginning
to talk of this and that, but then
after two minutes, off again,
they're on the dance-floor, waltzing, spinning.
All are dumbfounded. Lensky shies
away from trusting his own eyes.

XLII

Now the mazurka sounds. Its thunder
used in times past to ring a peal
that huge ballrooms vibrated under,
while floors would split from crash of heel,
and frames would shudder, windows tremble;
now things are changed, now we resemble
ladies who glide on waxed parquet.
Yet the mazurka keeps today
in country towns and suchlike places
its pristine charm: heeltaps, and leaps,
and whiskers – all of this it keeps
as fresh as ever, for its graces
are here untouched by fashion's reign,
our modern Russia's plague and bane.

XLIII

. . . .

[Petushkóv's nails and spurs are sounding
(that half-pay archivist); and bounding
Buyánov's heels have split the wood
and wrecked the flooring-boards for good;
there's crashing, rumbling, pounding, trotting;
the deeper in the wood, the more
the logs; the wild ones have the floor;
they're plunging, whirling, all but squatting.
Ah, gently, gently, easy goes –
your heels will squash the ladies' toes!]

XLIV

Buyánov, my vivacious cousin,
leads Olga and Tatyana on
to Eugene; nineteen to the dozen,
Eugene takes Olga, and is gone;
he steers her, nonchalantly gliding,
he stoops and, tenderly confiding,
whispers some ballad of the hour,
squeezes her hand – and brings to flower
on her smug face a flush of pleasure.
Lensky has watched: his rage has blazed,
he's lost his self-command, and crazed
with jealousy beyond all measure
insists, when the mazurka ends,
on the cotillion, as amends.

XLV

He asks. She can't accept. Why ever?
No, she's already pledged her word
to Evgeny. Oh, God, she'd never ...
How could she? why, he'd never heard ...
scarce out of bibs, already fickle,
fresh from the cot, an infant pickle,
already studying to intrigue,
already high in treason's league!
He finds the shock beyond all bearing;
so, cursing women's devious course,
he leaves the house, calls for his horse
and gallops. Pistols made for pairing
and just a double charge of shot
will in a flash decide his lot.

CHAPTER SIX

La, sotto giorni nubilosi e brevi,
Nasce una gente a cui 'l morir non dole.

PETRARCH

I

Seeing Vladimir had defected,
Eugene, at Olga's side, was racked
by fresh *ennui* as he reflected
with pleasure on his vengeful act.
Olinka yawned, just like her neighbour,
and looked for Lensky, while the labour
of the cotillion's endless theme
oppressed her like a heavy dream.
It's over. Supper is proceeding.
Beds are made up; the guests are all
packed from the maids' wing to the hall.
Each one by now is badly needing
a place for rest. Eugene alone
has driven off, to find his own.

II

All sleep: from the saloon a roaring
proclaims where ponderous Pústyakov
beside his heavier half is snoring.
Gvozdín, Buyánov, Petushkóv
and Flyánov, amply lubricated,
on dining-chairs are all prostrated;
the floor serves Triquet for his nap,
in flannel, and an old fur cap.
In the two sisters' rooms extended,
the maidens all are slumbering deep.
Only Tatyana does not sleep,
but at the window, in the splendid
radiance of Dian, sits in pain
and looks out on the darkened plain.

III

His unexpected apparition,
the fleeting tenderness that stole
into his look, the exhibition
with Olga, all have pierced her soul;
she can't make out a single fraction
of his intent; and a reaction
of jealousy has made her start,
as if a cold hand squeezed her heart,
as if beneath her, dark and rumbling,
a gulf has gaped ... Says Tanya: 'I
am doomed to perish, yet to die
through him is sweetness' self. In grumbling
I find no sense; the truth is this,
it's not in him to bring me bliss.'

But onward, onward with my story!
A new acquaintance claims our quill.
Five versts or so from Krasnogórie,
Lensky's estate, there lives and still
thrives to this moment, in a station
of philosophic isolation,
Zarétsky, sometime king of brawls
and hetman of the gambling-halls,
arch-rake, pothouse tribune-persona,
but now grown plain and kind in stead,
paterfamilias (unwed),
unswerving friend, correct landowner,
and even honourable man:
so, if we want to change, we can!

The world of fashion, prone to flatter,
praised his fierce courage in its day:
true, with a pistol he could shatter
an ace a dozen yards away;
it's also true, in battle's rapture,
the circumstances of his capture
had made his name, when, bold as bold,
down from his Kalmuck steed he rolled
into the mud, a drunken goner,
and taken by the French – some prize! –
resigned himself to prison's ties,
like Regulus, that god of honour,
in order daily, chez Véry,
to drain, on credit, bottles three.

VI

Time was, he'd been the wittiest ever,
so brilliantly he'd hoax the fools,
so gloriously he'd fool the clever,
using overt or covert rules.
Sometimes his tricks would earn him trouble,
or cause the bursting of his bubble,
sometimes he'd fall into a trap
himself just like a simple chap.
But he could draw a joking moral,
return an answer, blunt or keen,
use cunning silence as a screen,
or cunningly create a quarrel,
get two young friends to pick a fight,
and put them on a paced-out site.

VII

Or he knew how to reconcile them
so that all three went off to lunch,
then later slyly he'd revile them
with lies and jokes that packed a punch;
sed alia tempora! The devil
(like passion's dream, that other revel)
goes out of us when youth is dead.
So my Zaretsky, as I said,
beneath bird-cherries and acacias
has found a port for his old age,
and lives, a veritable sage,
for planting cabbage, like Horatius,
and breeding ducks and geese as well,
and teaching children how to spell.

VIII

He was no fool; appreciated
by my Eugene, not for his heart,
but for the effect that he created
of sense and judgement. For his part
his converse gave Onegin pleasure;
so it was not in any measure,
the morning after, a surprise
when our Zaretsky met his eyes.
His visitor from the beginning
broke greetings off, and gave Eugene
a note from Lensky; in between
Zaretsky watched, and stood there grinning.
Onegin without more ado
crossed to the window, read it through.

IX

Pleasant, in spite of its compression,
gentlemanly, quite precise,
Vladimir's challenge found expression
that, though polite, was clear as ice.
Eugene's response was automatic;
he informed this envoy diplomatic
in terms where not a word was spared:
at any time he'd be prepared.
Zaretsky rose without discussion;
he saw no point in staying on,
with work at home; but when he'd gone,
Evgeny, whom the repercussion
left quite alone with his own soul,
was far from happy with his role.

X

With reason, too: for when he'd vetted
in secret judgement what he'd done,
he found too much that he regretted:
last night he'd erred in making fun,
so heartless and so detrimental,
of love so timorous and gentle.
In second place the poet might
have been a fool; yet he'd a right,
at eighteen years, to some compassion.
Evgeny loved him from his heart,
and should have played a different part:
no softball for the winds of fashion,
no boy, to fight or take offence –
the *man* of honour and of sense.

XI

He could have spoken without harming,
need not have bristled like a beast;
he should have settled for disarming
that youthful heart. 'But now at least
it's late, time's passing ... not to mention,
in our affair, the intervention
of that old duellistic fox,
that wicked, loose-tongue chatterbox ...
True, scorn should punish and should bridle
his wit, according to the rules
but whispers, the guffaw of fools ...'
Public opinion – here's our idol,
the spring of honour, and the pin
on which the world is doomed to spin.

XII

Lensky at home awaits the answer,
impatient, hatred flaming high;
but here comes our loud-talking prancer
who swaggers in with the reply.
The jealous poet's gloom is lightened!
knowing the offender, he'd been frightened
lest he should by some clever trick
avert his chest from pistol's click,
smooth his way out with humour's ointment.
But now Vladimir's doubts are still:
early tomorrow at the mill
before first light they have appointment,
to raise the safety catch and strain
to hit the target: thigh or brain.

XIII

Still blazing with resentment's fuel,
and set on hating the coquette,
Lensky resolved before the duel
not to see Olga; in a fret
watched sun and clock – then by such labours
defeated, turned up at his neighbour's.
He thought that Olga'd be confused,
struck down as if she'd been accused,
when he arrived; not in the slightest:
just as she'd always been, she tripped
to meet the unhappy poet, skipped
down from the porch, light as the lightest,
the giddiest hope, carefree and gay,
the same as any other day.

XIV

'Last night, what made you fly so early?'
was the first thing that Olga said.
All Lensky's thoughts went hurly-burly,
and silently he hung his head.
Rage died, and jealousy's obsession,
before such candour of expression,
such frank *tendresse*; away they stole
before such playfulness of soul! . . .
he looks, in sweet irresolution,
and then concludes: she loves him yet!
Already borne down by regret,
he almost begs for absolution,
he trembles, knows not what to tell;
he's happy, yes, he's almost well . . .

(XV, XVI,) XVII

Now brooding thoughts hold his attention
once more, at that beloved sight,
and so he lacks the strength to mention
the happenings of the previous night;
he murmurs: 'Olga's mine for saving;
I'll stop that tempter from depraving
her youth with all his repertoire
of sighs, and compliments, and fire;
that poisonous worm, despised, degrading,
shall not attack my lily's root;
I'll save this blossom on the shoot,
still hardly opened up, from fading.'
Friends, all this meant was: I've a date
for swapping bullets with my mate.

XVIII

If only Lensky'd known the burning
wound that had seared my Tanya's heart!
If Tanya'd had the chance of learning
that Lensky and Eugene, apart,
would settle, on the morrow morning,
for which of them the tomb was yawning,
perhaps her love could in the end
have reunited friend to friend!
But, even by accident, her passion
was undiscovered to that day.
Onegin had no word to say;
Tatyana pined in secret fashion:
of the whole world, her nurse alone,
if not slow-witted, might have known.

XIX

Lensky all evening, in distraction,
would talk, keep silent, laugh, then frown –
the quintessential reaction
of Muses' offspring; sitting down
before the clavichord with knitted
forehead, he strummed, his vision flitted
to Olga's face, he whispered low
'I think I'm happy.' Time to go,
the hour was late. And now from aching
the heart inside him seemed to shrink;
parting with Olga made him think
it was quite torn in half and breaking.
She faced him, questioning: 'But you? . . .'
'It's nothing.' And away he flew.

XX

Once home, he brought out and inspected
his pistols, laid them in their case,
undressed, by candlelight selected
and opened Schiller . . . but the embrace
of one sole thought holds him in keeping
and stops his doleful heart from sleeping:
Olga is there, he sees her stand
in untold beauty close at hand.
Vladimir shuts the book, for writing
prepares himself; and then his verse,
compact of amorous trash, and worse,
flows and reverberates. Reciting,
he sounds, in lyric frenzy sunk,
like Delvig when he's dining drunk.

XXI

By chance those verses haven't vanished;
I keep them, and will quote them here:
'Whither, oh whither are ye banished,
my golden days when spring was dear?
What fate is my tomorrow brewing?
the answer's past all human viewing,
it's hidden deep in gloom and dust.
No matter; fate's decree is just.
Whether the arrow has my number,
whether it goes careering past,
all's well; the destined hour at last
comes for awakening, comes for slumber;
blessed are daytime's care and cark,
blest is the advent of the dark!

XXII

'The morning star will soon be shining,
and soon will day's bright tune be played;
but I perhaps will be declining
into the tomb's mysterious shade;
the trail the youthful poet followed
by sluggish Lethe may be swallowed,
and I be by the world forgot;
but, lovely maiden, wilt thou not
on my untimely urn be weeping,
thinking: he loved me, and in strife
the sad beginnings of his life
he consecrated to my keeping? ...
Friend of my heart, be at my side,
beloved friend, thou art my bride!'

XXIII

So Lensky wrote, obscurely, limply
(in the romantic style, we say,
though what's romantic here I simply
fail to perceive – that's by the way).
At last, with dawn upon him, stooping
his weary head, and softly drooping
over the modish word *ideal*,
he dozed away; but when the real
magic of sleep had started claiming
its due oblivion, in the hush
his neighbour entered at a rush
and wakened Lensky by exclaiming:
'Get up: it's gone six! I'll be bound,
Onegin's waiting on the ground.'

XXIV

But he's mistaken: Eugene's lying
and sleeping sounder than a rock.
By now the shades of night are flying,
Vesper is met by crow of cock –
Onegin still is slumbering deeply.
By now the sun is climbing steeply,
and little dancing whirls of snow
glitter and tumble as they go,
but Eugene hasn't moved; for certain
slumber still floats above his head.
At last he wakes, and stirs in bed,
and parts the fringes of his curtain;
he looks, and sees the hour of day –
high time he should be on his way.

XXV

He rings at once, and what a scurry!
his French valet, Guillot, is there
with gown and slippers; tearing hurry,
as linen's brought for him to wear.
And while with all despatch he's dressing
he warns his man for duty, stressing
that with him to the trysting-place
he has to bring the battle-case.
By now the sledge is at the portal –
he's racing millward like a bird.
Arrived apace, he gives the word
to bring across Lepage's mortal
barrels, and then to drive aside
by two small oaktrees in a ride.

XXVI

While Lensky'd long been meditating
impatiently on the mill-dam,
Zaretsky, engineer-in-waiting,
condemned the millstones as a sham.
Onegin comes, and makes excuses;
but in Zaretsky he induces
amazement: 'Where's your second gone?'
In duels a pedantic don,
methodical by disposition,
a classicist, he'll not allow
that one be shot just anyhow –
only by rule, and strict tradition
inherited from earlier days
(for which he must receive due praise).

XXVII

Evgeny echoed him: 'My second?
He's here – Monsieur Guillot, my friend.
I had most surely never reckoned
his choice could shock or might offend;
though he's unknown, there's no suggestion
that he's not honest past all question.'
Zaretsky bit his lip. Eugene
asked Lensky: 'Should we start, I mean?'
Vladimir to this casual mention
replies: 'We might as well.' They walk
behind the mill. In solemn talk,
Zaretsky draws up a convention
with Guillot; while pourparlers last
the two foes stand with eyes downcast.

XXVIII

Foes! Is it long since from each other
the lust for blood drew them apart?
long since, like brother linked to brother,
they shared their days in deed and heart,
their table, and their hours of leisure?
But now, in this vindictive pleasure
hereditary foes they seem,
and as in some appalling dream
each coldly plans the other's slaughter . . .
could they not laugh out loud, before
their hands are dipped in scarlet gore,
could they not give each other quarter
and part in kindness? Just the same,
all modish foes dread worldly shame.

XXIX

Pistols are out, they gleam, the hammer
thumps as the balls are pressed inside
faceted muzzles by the rammer;
with a first click, the catch is tried.
Now powder's greyish stream is slipping
into the pan. Securely gripping,
the jagged flint's pulled back anew.
Guillot, behind a stump in view,
stands in dismay and indecision.
And now the two opponents doff
their cloaks; Zaretsky's measured off
thirty-two steps with great precision,
and on their marks has made them stand;
each grips his pistol in his hand.

XXX

'Now march.' And calmly, not yet seeking
to aim, at steady, even pace
the foes, cold-blooded and unspeaking,
each took four steps across the space,
four fateful stairs. Then, without slowing
the level tenor of his going,
Evgeny quietly began
to lift his pistol up. A span
of five more steps they went, slow-gaited,
and Lensky, left eye closing, aimed –
but just then Eugene's pistol flamed . . .
The clock of doom had struck as fated;
and the poet, without a sound,
let fall his pistol on the ground.

XXXI

Vladimir drops, hand softly sliding
to heart. And in his misted gaze
is death, not pain. So gently gliding
down slopes of mountains, when a blaze
of sunlight makes it flash and crumble,
a block of snow will slip and tumble.
Onegin, drenched with sudden chill,
darts to the boy, and looks, and still
calls out his name . . . All unavailing:
the youthful votary of rhyme
has found an end before his time.
The storm is over, dawn is paling,
the bloom has withered on the bough;
the altar flame's extinguished now.

XXXII

He lay quite still, and strange as dreaming
was that calm brow of one who swooned.
Shot through below the chest – and streaming
the blood came smoking from the wound.
A moment earlier, inspiration
had filled this heart, and detestation
and hope and passion; life had glowed
and blood had bubbled as it flowed;
but now the mansion is forsaken;
shutters are up, and all is pale
and still within, behind the veil
of chalk the window-panes have taken.
The lady of the house has fled.
Where to, God knows. The trail is dead.

XXXIII

With a sharp epigram it's pleasant
to infuriate a clumsy foe;
and, as observer, to be present
and watch him stubbornly bring low
his thrusting horns, and as he passes
blush to descry in looking-glasses
his foolish face; more pleasant yet
to hear him howl: 'that's me!' You'll get
more joy still when with mute insistence
you help him to an honoured fate
by calmly aiming at his pate
from any gentlemanly distance;
but when you've managed his despatch
you won't find that quite so much catch . . .

XXXIV

What if your pistol-shot has smitten
a friend of yours in his first youth
because some glance of his has bitten
your pride, some answer, or in truth
some nonsense thrown up while carousing,
or if himself, with rage arousing,
he's called you out – say, in your soul
what feelings would assume control
if, motionless, no life appearing,
death on his brow, your friend should lie,
stiffening as the hours go by,
before you on the ground, unhearing,
unspeaking, too, but stretched out there
deaf to the voice of your despair?

XXXV

Giving his pistol-butt a squeezing,
Evgeny looks at Lensky, chilled
at heart by grim remorse's freezing.
'Well, what?' the neighbour says, 'he's killed.'
Killed! . . . At this frightful word a-quiver,
Onegin turns, and with a shiver
summons his people. On the sleigh
with care Zaretsky stows away
the frozen corpse, drives off, and homing
vanishes with his load of dread.
The horses, as they sense the dead,
have snorted, reared, and whitely foaming
have drenched the steel bit as they go
and flown like arrows from a bow.

XXXVI

My friends, the bard stirs your compassion:
right in the flower of joyous hope,
hope that he's had no time to fashion
for men to see, still in the scope
of swaddling clothes – already blighted!
Where is the fire that once ignited,
where's the high aim, the ardent sense
of youth, so tender, so intense?
and where is love's tempestuous yearning,
where are the reveries this time,
the horror of disgrace and crime,
the thirst for work, the lust for learning,
and life celestial's phantom gleams,
stuff of the poet's hallowed dreams!

XXXVII

Perhaps to improve the world's condition,
perhaps for fame, he was endowed;
his lyre, now stilled, in its high mission
might have resounded long and loud
for aeons. Maybe it was fated
that on the world's staircase there waited
for him a lofty stair. His shade,
after the martyr's price it paid,
maybe bore off with it for ever
a secret truth, and at our cost
a life-creating voice was lost;
to it the people's blessing never
will reach, and past the tomb's compound
hymns of the ages never sound.

(XXXVIII,) XXXIX

Perhaps however, to be truthful,
he would have found a normal fate.
The years would pass; no longer youthful,
he'd see his soul cool in its grate;
his nature would be changed and steadied,
he'd sack the Muses and get wedded;
and in the country, blissful, horned,
in quilted dressing-gown adorned,
life's real meaning would have found him;
at forty he'd have got the gout,
drunk, eaten, yawned, grown weak and stout,
at length, midst children swarming round him,
midst crones with endless tears to shed,
and doctors, he'd have died in bed.

XL

Reader, whatever fate's direction,
we weep for the young lover's end,
the man of reverie and reflection,
the poet struck down by his friend!
Left-handed from the habitation
where dwelt this child of inspiration,
two pines have tangled at the root;
beneath, a brook rolls its tribute
toward the neighbouring valley's river.
The ploughman there delights to doze,
girl reapers as the streamlet flows
dip in their jugs; where shadows quiver
darkly above the water's lilt,
a simple monument is built.

XLI

Below it, when spring rains are swishing,
when, on the plain, green herbs are massed,
the shepherd sings of Volga's fishing
and plaits a piebald shoe of bast;
and the young city-bred newcomer,
who in the country spends her summer,
when galloping at headlong pace
alone across the fields of space,
will halt her horse and, gripping tightly
the leather rein, to learn the tale,
lift up the gauzes of her veil,
with a quick look perusing lightly
the simple legend – then a haze
of tears will cloud her tender gaze.

XLII

Walking her horse in introspection
across the plain's enormous room,
what holds her in profound reflection,
despite herself, is Lensky's doom;
'Olga,' she thinks, 'what fate befell her?
her heartache, did it long compel her,
or did her grief soon find repair?
and where's her sister now? and where,
flown from society as we know it,
of modish belles the modish foe,
where did that glum eccentric go,
the one who killed the youthful poet?'
All in good time, on each point I
will give you a complete reply.

XLIII

But not today. Although I dearly
value the hero of my tale,
though I'll come back to him, yet clearly
to face him now I feel too frail ...
The years incline to gloom and prosing,
they kill the zest of rhymed composing,
and with a sigh I now admit
I have to drag my feet to it.
My pen, as once, no longer hurries
to spoil loose paper by the ream;
another, a more chilling dream,
and other, more exacting worries,
in fashion's din, at still of night,
come to disturb me and affright.

XLIV

I've learnt the voice of new ambition,
I've learnt new sadness; but in this
the first will never find fruition,
the earlier griefs are what I miss.
O dreams, o dreams, where is your sweetness?
where (standard rhyme) are youth
    and fleetness?
can it be true, their crown at last
has felt time's desiccating blast?
can it be true, and firmly stated
without an elegiac frill,
that spring with me has had its fill
(as I've so oft in jest related)?
Can it be true, it won't come twice –
and I'll be thirty in a trice?

XLV

Well, I must make a frank confession,
my noon is here, and that's the truth.
So let me with a kind expression
take leave of my lightheaded youth!
Thank you for all the gifts I treasure,
thank you for sorrow and for pleasure,
thank you for suffering and its joys,
for tempests and for feasts and noise;
thank you indeed. Alike in sorrow
and in flat calm I've found the stuff
of perfect bliss in you. Enough!
My soul's like crystal, and tomorrow
I shall set out on brand-new ways
and rest myself from earlier days.

XLVI

Let me look back. Farewell, umbrageous
forests where my young age was passed
in indolence and in rampageous
passion and dreams of pensive cast.
But come, thou youthful inspiration,
come, trouble my imagination,
liven the drowsing of my heart,
fly to my corner like a dart,
let not the poet's soul of passion
grow cold, and hard, and stiff as stock,
and finally be turned to rock
amid the deadening joys of fashion,
[amongst the soulless men of pride,
the fools who sparkle far and wide,

XLVII

amongst the crafty and small-minded,
the children spoilt, the mad, the rogues
both dull and ludicrous, the blinded
critics and their capricious vogues,
amongst devout coquettes, appalling
lickspittles who adore their crawling,
and daily scenes of modish life
where civil treacheries are rife,
urbane betrayals, and the chilling
verdicts of vanity the bleak,
men's thoughts, their plots, the words
        they speak,
all of an emptiness so killing —]
that's the morass, I beg you note,
in which, dear friends, we're all afloat!

CHAPTER SEVEN

Moscow, loved daughter of Russia,
where can we find your equal?
DMITRIEV

'How can one not love mother Moscow?'
BARATYNSKY

'You criticize Moscow? why make such a fuss of
seeing the world? what on earth could be better?'
'A place where you'll find none of us.'
GRIBOEDOV

I

By now the rays of spring are chasing
the snow from all surrounding hills;
it melts, away it rushes, racing
down to the plain in turbid rills.
Smiling through sleep, nature is meeting
the infant year with cheerful greeting:
the sky is brilliant in its blue
and, still transparent to the view,
the downy woods are greener-tinted;
from waxen cell the bees again
levy their tribute on the plain;
the vales dry out, grow brightly printed;
cows low, in the still nights of spring
the nightingale's begun to sing.

II

O spring! o time for love! how sadly
your advent swamps me in its flood!
and in my soul, o spring, how madly
your presence aches, and in my blood!
How heavy, and how near to sobbing,
the bliss that fills me when your throbbing,
caressing breath has fanned my face
in rural calm's most secret place!
Or from all notion of enjoyment
am I estranged, does all that cheers,
that lives, and glitters, and endears,
now crush with sorrow's dull deployment
a soul that perished long ago,
and finds the world a darkling show?

III

Or, unconsoled by the returning
of leaves that autumn killed for good,
are we recalled to grief still burning
by the new whisper in the wood?
or else does nature, fresh and staring,
set off our troubled mind comparing
its newness with our faded days,
with years no more to meet our gaze?
Perhaps, when thoughts are all a-quiver
in midst of a poetic dream,
some other, older spring will gleam,
and put our heart into a shiver
with visions of enchanted night,
of distant countries, of moonlight . . .

IV

It's time: kind-hearted, idle creatures,
dons of Epicurean rule,
calm men with beatific features,
graduates of the Levshin school,
Priam-like agricultural sages,
sensitive ladies of all ages –
the spring invites you to the land
now warmth and blossom are on hand,
field-work, and walks with inspiration,
and magic nights. In headlong course
come to the fields, my friends! To horse!
With mounts from home, or postal station,
in loaded carriages, migrate,
leave far behind that city-gate.

V

Forsake, indulgent reader – driven
in your *calèche* of foreign cast –
the untiring city, where you've given
to feasts and fun this winter past;
and though my muse may be capricious,
we'll go with her to that delicious
and nameless rivulet, that scene
of whispering woods where my Eugene,
an idle monk in glum seclusion,
has lately wintered, just a space
from young Tatyana's dwelling-place,
dear Tanya, lover of illusion;
though there he's no more to be found,
he's left sad footprints on the ground.

VI

Amidst the hills, down in that valley,
let's go where, winding all the time
across green meadows, dilly-dally,
a brook flows through a grove of lime.
There sings the nightingale, spring's lover,
the wild rose blooms, and in the covert
the source's chattering voice is heard;
and there a tombstone says its word
where two old pinetrees stand united:
'This is Vladimir Lensky's grave
who early died as die the brave' –
the headpiece-text is thus indited –
the year, his age, then: 'may your rest,
young poet, be for ever blest!'

VII

There was a pine-branch downward straying
towards the simple urn beneath;
time was when morning's breeze was swaying
over it a mysterious wreath:
time was, in evening hours of leisure,
by moonlight two young girls took pleasure,
closely embraced, in wending here,
to see the grave, and shed a tear.
Today . . . the sad memorial's lonely,
forgot. Its trodden path is now
choked up. There's no wreath on the bough;
grey-haired and weak, beneath it only
the shepherd, as he used to do,
sings as he plaits a humble shoe.

(VIII, IX,) X

Poor Lensky! Set aside for weeping,
or pining, Olga's hours were brief.
Alas for him! there was no keeping
his sweetheart faithful to her grief.
Another had the skill to ravish
her thoughts away, knew how to lavish
sweet words by which her pain was banned –
a Lancer wooed and won her hand,
a Lancer – how she deified him!
and at the altar, with a crown,
her head in modesty cast down,
already there she stands beside him;
her eyes are lowered, but ablaze,
and on her lips a light smile plays.

XI

Poor Lensky! where the tomb is bounded
by dull eternity's purlieus,
was the sad poet not confounded
at this betrayal's fateful news?
Or, as by Lethe's bank he slumbered,
perhaps no more sensations lumbered
the lucky bard, and as he dozed
the earth for him grew dumb and closed? . . .
On such indifference, such forgetting
beyond the grave we all must build –
foes, friends and loves, their voice is stilled.
Only the estate provides a setting
for angry heirs, as one, to fall
into an unbecoming brawl.

XII

Presently Olga's ringing answer
inside the Larins' house fell mute.
Back to his regiment the Lancer,
slave of the service, was *en route*.
Weltered in tears, and sorely smarting,
the old dame wept her daughter's parting,
and in her grief seemed fit to die;
but Tanya found she couldn't cry:
only the pallor of heart-breaking
covered her face. When all came out
onto the porch, and fussed about
over the business of leave-taking,
Tatyana went with them, and sped
the carriage of the newly-wed.

XIII

And long, as if through mists that spurted,
Tanya pursued them with her gaze . . .
So there she stood, forlorn, deserted!
The comrade of so many days,
oh! her young dove, the natural hearer
of secrets, like a friend but dearer,
had been for ever borne off far
and parted from her by their star.
Shade-like, in purposeless obsession
she roams the empty garden-plot . . .
in everything she sees there's not
a grain of gladness; tears' repression
allows no comfort to come through –
Tatyana's heart is rent in two.

XIV

Her passion burns with stronger powder
now she's bereft, and just the same
her heart speaks to her even louder
of far-away Onegin's name.
She'll not see him, her obligation
must be to hold in detestation
the man who laid her brother low.
The poet's dead . . . already though
no one recalls him or his verses;
by now his bride-to-be has wed
another, and his memory's fled
as smoke in azure sky disperses.
Two hearts there are perhaps that keep
a tear for him . . . but what's to weep?

XV

Evening, and darkening sky, and waters
in quiet flood. A beetle whirred.
The choirs of dancers sought their quarters.
Beyond the stream there smoked and stirred
a fisher's fire. Through country gleaming
silver with moonlight, in her dreaming
profoundly sunk, Tatyana stalked
for hours alone; she walked and walked . . .
Suddenly, from a crest, she sighted
a house, a village, and a wood
below a hill; a garden stood
above a stream the moon had lighted.
She looked across, felt in her heart
a faster, stronger pulsing start.

XVI

She hesitates, and doubts beset her:
forward or back? it's true that he
has left, and no one here has met her . . .
'The house, the park . . . I'll go and see!'
So down came Tanya, hardly daring
to draw a breath, around her staring
with puzzled and confused regard . . .
She entered the deserted yard.
Dogs, howling, rushed in her direction . . .
Her frightened cry brought running out
the household boys in noisy rout;
giving the lady their protection,
by dint of cuff and kick and smack
they managed to disperse the pack.

XVII

'Could I just see the house, I wonder?'
Tatyana asked. The children all
rushed to Anisia's room, to plunder
the keys that opened up the hall.
At once Anisia came to greet her,
the doorway opened wide to meet her,
she went inside the empty shell
in which our hero used to dwell.
She looks: forgotten past all chalking
on billiard-table rests a cue,
and on the crumpled sofa too
a riding whip. Tanya keeps walking . . .
'And here's the hearth,' explains the crone,
'where master used to sit alone.

XVIII

'Here in the winter he'd have dinner
with neighbour Lensky, the deceased.
Please follow me. And here's the inner
study where he would sleep and feast
on cups of coffee, and then later
he'd listen to the administrator;
in morning time he'd read a book . . .
And just here, in the window-nook,
is where old master took up station,
and put his glasses on to see
his Sunday game of cards with me.
I pray God grant his soul salvation,
and rest his dear bones in the tomb,
down in our damp earth-mother's womb!'

XIX

Tatyana in a deep emotion
gazes at all the scene around;
she drinks it like a priceless potion;
it stirs her drooping soul to bound
in fashion that's half-glad, half-anguished:
that table where the lamp has languished,
beside the window-sill, that bed
on which a carpet has been spread,
piled books, and through the pane the sable
moonscape, the half-light overall,
Lord Byron's portrait on the wall,
the iron figure on the table,
the hat, the scowling brow, the chest
where folded arms are tightly pressed.

XX

Longtime inside this modish cloister,
as if spellbound, Tatyana stands.
It's late. A breeze begins to roister,
the valley's dark. The forest lands
round the dim river sleep; the curtain
of hills has hid the moon; for certain
the time to go has long since passed
for the young pilgrim. So at last
Tatyana, hiding her condition,
and not without a sigh, perforce
sets out upon her homeward course;
before she goes, she seeks permission
to come back to the hall alone
and read the books there on her own.

XXI

Outside the gate Tatyana parted
with old Anisia. The next day
at earliest morning out she started,
to the empty homestead made her way,
then in the study's quiet setting,
at last alone, and quite forgetting
the world and all its works, she wept
and sat there as the minutes crept;
the books then underwent inspection ...
at first she had no heart to range;
but then she found their choice was strange.
To reading from this odd collection
Tatyana turned with thirsting soul:
and watched a different world unroll.

XXII

Though long since Eugene's disapproval
had ruled out reading, in their place
and still exempted from removal
a few books had escaped disgrace:
Don Juan's and the Giaour's creator,
two or three novels where our later
epoch's portrayed, survived the ban,
works where contemporary man
is represented rather truly,
that soul without a moral tie,
all egoistical and dry,
to dreaming given up unduly,
and that embittered mind which boils
in empty deeds and futile toils.

XXIII

There many pages keep the impression
where a sharp nail has made a dent.
On these, with something like obsession,
the girl's attentive eyes are bent.
Tatyana sees with trepidation
what kind of thought, what observation,
had drawn Eugene's especial heed
and where he'd silently agreed.
Her eyes along the margin flitting
pursue his pencil. Everywhere
Onegin's soul encountered there
declares itself in ways unwitting –
terse words or crosses in the book,
or else a query's wondering hook.

XXIV

And so, at last, feature by feature,
Tanya begins to understand
more thoroughly, thank God, the creature
for whom her passion has been planned
by fate's decree: this freakish stranger,
who walks with sorrow, and with danger,
whether from heaven or from hell,
this angel, this proud devil, tell,
what is he? Just an apparition,
a shadow, null and meaningless,
a Muscovite in Harold's dress,
a modish second-hand edition,
a glossary of smart *argot* ...
a parodistic raree-show?

XXV

Can she have found the enigma's setting?
is this the riddle's missing clue?
Time races, and she's been forgetting
her journey home is overdue.
Some neighbours there have come together;
they talk of her, of how and whether:
'Tanya's no child – it's past a joke,'
says the old lady in a croak:
'why, Olga's younger, and she's bedded.
It's time she went. But what can I
do with her when a flat reply
always comes back: I'll not be wedded.
And then she broods and mopes for good,
and trails alone around the wood.'

XXVI

'She's not in love?' 'There's no one, ever.
Buyánov tried – got flea in ear.
And Ivan Petushkóv; no, never.
Pikhtín, of the Hussars, was here;
he found Tatyana so attractive,
bestirred himself, was devilish active!
I thought, she'll go this time, perhaps;
far from it! just one more collapse.'
'You don't see what to do? that's funny:
Moscow's the place, the marriage-fair!
There's vacancies in plenty there.'
'My dear good sir, I'm short of money.'
'One winter's worth, you've surely got;
or borrow, say, from me, if not.'

XXVII

The old dame had no thought of scouting
such good and sensible advice;
accounts were done, a winter outing
to Moscow settled in a trice.
Then Tanya hears of the decision.
To face society's derision
with the unmistakeable sideview
of a provincial *ingénue*,
to expose to Moscow fops and Circes
her out-of-fashion turns of phrase,
parade before their mocking gaze
her out-of-fashion clothes! . . . oh, mercies!
no, forests are the sole retreat
where her security's complete.

XXVIII

Risen with earliest rays of dawning,
Tanya today goes hurrying out
into the fields, surveys the morning,
with deep emotion looks about
and says: 'Farewell, you vales and fountains!
farewell you too, familiar mountains!
Farewell, familiar woods! Farewell,
beauty with all its heavenly spell,
gay nature and its sparkling distance!
This dear, still world I must forswear
for vanity, and din, and glare! . . .
Farewell to you, my free existence!
whither does all my yearning tend?
my fate, it leads me to what end?'

XXIX

She wanders on without direction.
Often she halts against her will,
arrested by the sheer perfection
she finds in river and in hill.
As with old friends, she craves diversion
in gossip's rambling and discursion
with her own forests and her meads . . .
But the swift summer-time proceeds –
now golden autumn's just arriving.
Now Nature's tremulous, pale effect
suggests a victim richly decked . . .
The north wind blows, the clouds are driving –
amidst the howling and the blast
sorceress-winter's here at last.

XXX

She's here, she spreads abroad; she stipples
the branches of the oak with flock;
lies in a coverlet that ripples
across the fields, round hill and rock;
the bank, the immobile stream are levelled
beneath a shroud that's all dishevelled;
frost gleams. We watch with gleeful thanks
old mother winter at her pranks.
Only from Tanya's heart, no cheering –
for her, no joy from winter-time,
she won't inhale the powdered rime,
nor from the bath-house roof be clearing
first snow for shoulders, breast and head:
for Tanya, winter's ways are dread.

XXXI

Departure date's long overtaken;
at last the final hours arrive.
A sledded coach, for years forsaken,
relined and strengthened for the drive;
three carts – traditional procession –
with every sort of home possession:
pans, mattresses, and trunks, and chairs,
and jam in jars, and household wares,
and feather-beds, and birds in cages,
with pots and basins out of mind,
and useful goods of every kind.
There's din of parting now that rages,
with tears, in quarters of the maids:
and, in the yard, stand eighteen jades.

XXXII

Horses and coach are spliced in marriage;
the cooks prepare the midday meal;
mountains are piled on every carriage,
and coachmen swear, and women squeal.
The bearded outrider is sitting
his spindly, shaggy nag. As fitting,
to wave farewell the household waits
for the two ladies at the gates.
They're settled in; and crawling, sliding,
the grand barouche is on its way.
'Farewell, you realms that own the sway
of solitude, and peace abiding!
shall I see you?' As Tanya speaks
the tears in stream pour down her cheeks.

XXXIII

When progress and amelioration
have pushed their frontiers further out,
in time (to quote the calculation
of philosophic brains, about
five hundred years) for sure our byways
will blossom into splendid highways:
paved roads will traverse Russia's length
bringing her unity and strength;
and iron bridges will go arching
over the waters in a sweep;
mountains will part; below the deep,
audacious tunnels will be marching:
Godfearing folk will institute
an inn at each stage of the route.

XXXIV

But now our roads are bad, the ages
have gnawed our bridges, and the flea
and bedbug that infest the stages
allow no rest to you or me;
inns don't exist; but in a freezing
log cabin a pretentious-teasing
menu, hung up for show, excites
all sorts of hopeless appetites;
meanwhile the local Cyclops, aiming
a Russian hammer-blow, repairs
Europe's most finely chiselled wares
before a fire too slowly flaming,
and blesses the unrivalled brand
of ruts that grace our fatherland.

XXXV

By contrast, in the frozen season,
how pleasantly the stages pass.
Like modish rhymes that lack all reason,
the winter's ways are smooth as glass.
Then our Automedons are flashing,
our troikas effortlessly dashing,
and mileposts grip the idle sense
by flickering past us like a fence.
Worse luck, Larina crawled; the employment
of her own horses, not the post,
spared her the expense she dreaded most –
and gave our heroine enjoyment
of traveller's tedium at its peak:
their journey took them a full week.

XXXVI

But now they're near. Already gleaming
before their eyes they see unfold
the towers of whitestone Moscow beaming
with fire from every cross of gold.
Friends, how my heart would leap with
    pleasure
when suddenly I saw this treasure
of spires and belfries, in a cup
with parks and mansions, open up.
How often would I fall to musing
of Moscow in the mournful days
of absence on my wandering ways!
Moscow . . . how many strains are fusing
in that one sound, for Russian hearts!
what store of riches it imparts!

XXXVII

Here stands, with shady park surrounded,
Petrovsky Castle; and the fame
in which so lately it abounded
rings proudly in that sombre name.
Napoleon here, intoxicated
with recent fortune, vainly waited
till Moscow, meekly on its knees,
gave up the ancient Kremlin-keys:
but no, my Moscow never stumbled
nor crawled in suppliant attire.
No feast, no welcome-gifts – with fire
the impatient conqueror was humbled!
From here, deep-sunk in pensive woe,
he gazed out on the threatening glow.

XXXVIII

Farewell, Petrovsky Castle, glimmer
of fallen glory. Well! don't wait,
drive on! And now we see a-shimmer
the pillars of the turnpike-gate;
along Tverskaya Street already
the potholes make the coach unsteady.
Street lamps go flashing by, and stalls,
boys, country women, stately halls,
parks, monasteries, towers and ledges,
Bokharans, orchards, merchants, shacks,
boulevards, chemists, and Cossacks,
peasants, and fashion-shops, and sledges,
lions adorning gateway posts
and, on the crosses, jackdaw hosts.

(XXXIX,) XL

This wearisome perambulation
takes up an hour or two; at last
the coach has reached its destination;
after Saint Chariton's gone past
a mansion stands just round a turning.
On an old aunt, who's long been burning
with a consumption, they've relied.
And now the door is opened wide,
a grizzled Kalmuck stands to meet them,
bespectacled, in tattered dress;
and from the salon the princess,
stretched on a sofa, calls to greet them.
The two old ladies kiss and cry;
thickly the exclamations fly.

XLI

'Princess, *mon ange!*' 'Pachette!' 'Alina!'
'Who would have thought it?' 'What an age!'
'How long can you ...?' 'Dearest *kuzina!*'
'Sit down! how strange! it's like the stage
or else a novel.' 'And my daughter
Tatyana's here, you know I've brought her ...'
'Ah, Tanya, come to me, it seems
I'm wandering in a world of dreams ...
Grandison, cousin, d'you remember?'
'What, Grandison? oh, Grandison!
I do, I do. Well, where's he gone?'
'Here, near Saint Simeon; in December,
on Christmas Eve, he wished me joy:
lately he married off his boy.'

XLII

'As for the other one ... tomorrow
we'll talk, and talk, and then we'll show
Tanya to all her kin. My sorrow
is that my feet lack strength to go
outside the house. But you'll be aching
after your drive, it's quite back-breaking;
let's go together, take a rest ...
Oh, I've no strength ... I'm tired, my chest ...
These days I'm finding even gladness,
not only pain, too much to meet ...
I'm good for nothing now, my sweet ...
you age, and life's just grief and sadness ...'
With that, in tears, and quite worn out,
she burst into a coughing-bout.

XLIII

The invalid's glad salutation,
her kindness, move Tatyana; yet
the strangeness of her habitation,
after her own room, makes her fret.
No sleep, beneath that silken curtain,
in that new couch, no sleep for certain;
the early pealing of the bells
lifts her from bed as it foretells
the occupations of the morning.
She sits down by the window-sill.
The darkness thins away; but still
no vision of her fields is dawning.
An unknown yard, she sees from thence,
a stall, a kitchen and a fence.

XLIV

The kinsfolk in concerted action
ask Tanya out to dine, and they
present her languor and distraction
to fresh grandparents every day.
For cousins from afar, on meeting
there never fails a kindly greeting,
and exclamations, and good cheer.
'How Tanya's grown! I pulled your ear
just yesterday.' 'And since your christening
how long is it?' 'And since I fed
you in my arms on gingerbread?'
And all grandmothers who are listening
in unison repeat the cry:
'My goodness, how the years do fly!'

XLV

Their look, though, shows no change upon it –
they all still keep their old impress:
still made of tulle, the self-same bonnet
adorns Aunt Helen, the princess;
still powdered is Lukérya Lvovna,
a liar still, Lyubóv Petrovna,
Iván Petróvich still is dumb,
Semyón Petróvich, mean and glum,
and then old cousin Pelagéya
still has Monsieur Finemouche for friend,
same Pom, same husband to the end;
he's at the club, a real stayer,
still meek, still deaf as howd'youdo,
still eats and drinks enough for two.

XLVI

And in their daughters' close embraces
Tanya is gripped. No comment's made
at first by Moscow's youthful graces
while she's from top to toe surveyed;
they find her somewhat unexpected,
a bit provincial and affected,
too pale, too thin, but on the whole
not bad at all; and then each soul
gives way to nature's normal passion:
she's their great friend, asked in, caressed,
her hands affectionately pressed;
they fluff her curls out in the fashion,
and in a singsong voice confide
the inmost thoughts that girls can hide.

XLVII

Each others' and their own successes,
their hopes, their pranks, their dreams at night –
and so the harmless chat progresses
coated with a thin layer of spite.
Then in return for all this twaddle,
from her they strive to coax and coddle
a full confession of the heart.
Tatyana hears but takes no part;
as if she'd been profoundly sleeping,
there's not a word she's understood;
she guards, in silence and for good,
her sacred store of bliss and weeping
as something not to be declared,
a treasure never to be shared.

XLVIII

To talk, to general conversation
Tatyana seeks to attune her ear,
but the salon's preoccupation
is with dull trash that can't cohere:
everything's dim and unenthusing;
even the scandal's not amusing;
in talk, so fruitless and so stale,
in question, gossip, news and tale,
not once a day a thought will quiver,
not even by chance, once in a while,
will the benighted reason smile,
even in joke the heart won't shiver.
This world's so vacuous that it's got
no spark of fun in all its rot!

XLIX

In swarms around Tatyana ranging,
the modish Record Office clerks
stare hard at her before exchanging
some disagreeable remarks.
One melancholy fop, declaring
that she's 'ideal', begins preparing
an elegy to her address,
propped in the door among the press.
Once Vyázemsky, who chanced to find her
at some dull aunt's, sat down and knew
how to engage in talk that drew
her soul's attention; just behind her
an old man saw her as she came,
straightened his wig, and asked her name.

L

But where, mid tragic storms that rend her,
Melpomene wails long and loud,
and brandishes her tinsel splendour
before a cold, indifferent crowd,
and where Thalia, gently napping,
ignores approval's friendly clapping,
and where Terpsichore alone
moves the young watcher (as was known
to happen long ago, dear readers,
in our first ages), from no place
did any glasses seek her face,
lorgnettes of jealous fashion-leaders,
or quizzing-glasses of know-alls
in boxes or the rows of stalls.

LI

They take her too to the Assembly.
The crush, the heat, as music blares,
the blaze of candles, and the trembly
flicker of swiftly twirling pairs,
the beauties in their flimsy dresses,
the swarm, the glittering mob that presses,
the ring of marriageable girls –
bludgeon the sense; it faints and whirls.
Here insolent prize-dandies wither
all others with a waistcoat's set
and an insouciant lorgnette.
Hussars on leave are racing hither
to boom, to flash across the sky,
to captivate, and then to fly.

LII

The night has many stars that glitter,
Moscow has beauties and to spare;
but brighter than the heavenly litter,
the moon in its azure of air.
And yet that goddess whom I'd never
importune with my lyre, whenever
like a majestic moon, she drives
among the maidens and the wives,
how proudly, how divinely gleaming,
she treads our earth, and how her breast
is in voluptuous languor dressed,
how sensuously her eyes are dreaming!
Enough, I tell you, that will do –
you've paid insanity its due.

LIII

Noise, laughter, bowing, helter-skelter
galop, mazurka, waltz ... Meanwhile
between two aunts, in pillared shelter,
unnoticed, in unseeing style,
Tanya looks on; her own indictment
condemns the *monde* and its excitement;
she finds it stifling here ... she strains
in dream toward the woods and plains,
the country cottages and hovels,
and to that far and lonely nook
where flows a little glittering brook,
to her flower-garden, to her novels, –
to where *he* came to her that time
in twilight of *allées* of lime.

LIV

But while she roams in thought, not caring
for dance, and din, and worldly ways,
a general of majestic bearing
has fixed on her a steady gaze.
The aunts exchanged a look, they fluttered,
they nudged Tatyana, and each muttered
at the same moment in her ear:
'Look quickly to the left, d'you hear?'
'Look to the left? where? what's the matter?'
'There, just in front of all that swarm,
you see the two in uniform ...
just look, and never mind the chatter ...
he's moved ... you see him from the side.'
'Who? that fat general?' Tanya cried.

LV

But here, with our congratulation
on her conquest, we leave my sweet;
I'm altering my destination
lest in forgetfulness complete
I drop my hero ... I'll be truthful:
'It is a friend I sing, a youthful
amateur of caprice and quirk.
Muse of the epic, bless my work!
in my long task, be my upholder,
put a strong staff into my hand,
don't let me stray in paths unplanned.'
Enough. The load is off my shoulder!
I've paid my due to classic art:
it may be late, but it's a start.

CHAPTER EIGHT

Fare thee well, and if for ever,
Still for ever, fare thee well.

BYRON

I

Days when I came to flower serenely
in Lycée gardens long ago,
and read my Apuleius keenly,
but spared no glance for Cicero;
yes, in that spring-time, in low-lying
secluded vales, where swans were crying,
by waters that were still and clear,
for the first time the Muse came near.
And suddenly her radiance lighted
my student cell: she opened up
the joys of youth, that festal cup,
she sang of childhood's fun, indited
Russia's old glories and their gleams,
the heart and all its fragile dreams.

II

And with a smile the world caressed us:
what wings our first successes gave!
aged Derzhávin saw and blessed us
as he descended to the grave.

. . . .

III

The arbitrary rules of passion
were all the law that I would use;
sharing her in promiscuous fashion,
I introduced my saucy Muse
to roar of banquets, din of brawling,
when night patrol's a perilous calling;
to each and every raving feast
she brought her talents, never ceased,
Bacchante-like, her flighty prancing;
sang for the guests above the wine;
the youth of those past days in line
behind her followed wildly dancing;
among my friends, in all that crowd
my giddy mistress made me proud.

IV

When I defected from their union
and ran far off . . . the Muse came too.
How often, with her sweet communion,
she'd cheer my wordless way, and do
her secret work of magic suasion!
How often on the steep Caucasian
ranges, Lenora-like, she'd ride
breakneck by moonlight at my side!
How oft she'd lead me, by the Tauric
seacoast, to hear in dark of night
the murmuring Nereids recite,
and the deep-throated billows' choric
hymnal as, endlessly unfurled,
they praise the Father of the world.

V

But then, oblivious of the city,
its glaring feasts, and shrill events,
in far Moldavia, fit for pity,
she visited the humble tents
of wandering tribesmen; while the ravage
of their society turned her savage,
she lost the language of the gods
for the bleak tongue of boorish clods –
she loved the steppe-land and its singing . . .
then quickly something changed all this:
look here, as a provincial miss
she's turned up in my garden, bringing
sad meditations in her look,
and, in her hand, a small French book.

VI

Now for the first time she's escorted
into the social whirlabout;
jealously, shyly, I've imported
her steppeland charms into a *rout*.
Through the tight ranks — aristocratic,
military-foppish, diplomatic —
past the grand ladies, see her glide;
she sits down calmly on one side,
admires the tumult and the pressing,
the flickering tones of dress and speech,
the young hostess, towards whom each
new guest is gradually progressing,
while men, all sombre, all the same,
set off the ladies like a frame.

VII

She enjoys the stately orchestration
of oligarchical converse,
pride's icy calm, the combination
of ranks and ages so diverse.
But who stands there, in this selected
assembly, silent and dejected?
All who behold him find him strange.
Faces before him flash and change
like irksome phantoms, null as zero.
Is spleen his trouble, or the dumb
torment of pride? And why's he come?
Who on earth is he? not . . . our hero?
No doubt about it, it's Eugene.
'How long has he been on the scene?

VIII

'Still as he was? has he stopped prancing?
does he still pose, and play the freak?
Now he's returned, what role's he dancing?
what play will he present this week?
For what charade is he apparelled?
Is he a Melmoth, a Childe Harold,
a patriot, a cosmopolite,
bigot or prude? or has he quite
a different mask? is he becoming
someone like you and me, just nice?
At least I'll give him some advice:
to drop all that old-fashioned mumming;
too long he's hoaxed us high and low ...'
'You know him, do you?' 'Yes and no.'

IX

However has he earned so vicious,
so unforgiving a report?
Is it that we've become officious
and prone to censure in our thought;
that fiery souls' headstrong enthusing
appears offensive or amusing
to the complacent and the null;
that wit embarrasses the dull;
that we enjoy equating chatter
with deeds; that dunces now and then
take wing on spite; that serious men
find, in the trivial, serious matter;
that mediocre dress alone
fits us as if it were our own?

X

Blest he who in his youth was truly
youthful, who ripened in his time,
and, as the years went by, who duly
grew hardened to life's frosty clime;
who never learnt how dreamers babble;
who never scorned the social rabble;
at twenty, was a fop inbred,
at thirty, lucratively wed;
at fifty, would prolong the story
by clearing every sort of debt;
who, in good time, would calmly get
fortune, and dignity, and glory,
who all his life would garner praise
as the perfection of our days!

XI

Alas, *our* youth was what we made it,
something to fritter and to burn,
when hourly we ourselves betrayed it,
and it deceived us in return;
when our sublimest aspiration,
and all our fresh imagination,
swiftly decayed beyond recall
like foliage in the rotting fall.
It's agony to watch the hollow
sequence of dinners stretch away,
to see life as a ritual play,
and with the decorous throng to follow
although one in no manner shares
its views, its passions, or its cares!

XII

To be a butt for the malicious
is agony, if I may speak,
and in the eyes of the judicious
to pass for an affected freak,
or for a lamentable manic,
a monster of the *gens* Satanic,
or for that Demon of my dream.
Onegin – now once more my theme –
had killed his best friend in a duel;
without a goal on which to fix,
lived to the age of twenty-six;
was finding leisure's vacuum cruel;
and with no post, no work, no wife,
had nothing to employ his life.

XIII

He was the slave of a tenacious,
a restless urge for change of place
(an attribute that's quite vexatious,
though some support it with good grace).
He's gone away and left his village,
the solitude of woods and tillage,
where every day a bloodstained shade
had come to him in field and glade;
started a life of pointless roaming,
dogged by one feeling, only one –
and soon his travels had begun,
as all things did, to bore him; homing,
like Chatsky, he arrived to fall
direct from shipboard into ball.

XIV

There came a murmur, for a fleeting
moment the assembly seemed to shake ...
that lady the hostess was greeting,
with the grand general in her wake –
she was unhurried, unobtrusive,
not cold, but also not effusive,
no haughty stare around the press,
no proud pretentions to success,
no mannerism, no affectation,
no artifices of the vain ...
No, all in her was calm and plain.
She struck one as the incarnation –
Shishkov, forgive me: I don't know
the Russian for *le comme il faut*.

XV

Ladies came over, crossed to meet her,
dowagers smiled as she went by;
and bending deeply down to greet her
men made their bows, and sought her eye;
girls as they passed her spoke less loudly,
and no one in the room so proudly
raised nose and shoulders high and wide
as did the general at her side.
You'd never class her as a beauty;
and yet in her you'd not detect –
rigorously though you'd inspect –
what London calls, with humble duty
to fashion's absolute dictate,
a *vulgar* touch. I can't translate.

XVI

And yet, although it's past conveying,
I really dote upon the word:
it's new to us, beyond gainsaying;
from the first moment it was heard
it had its epigram-potential ...
But let's return to our essential,
that lady whose engaging charm
so effortlessly can disarm.
She sits with Nina at a table –
bright Northern Cleopatra she:
but you'll undoubtedly agree
that marble Nina's proved unable
to steal away her neighbour's light
or dim her, dazzle as she might.

XVII

'Can it be she?' Eugene in wonder
demanded. 'Yes, she looks ... And yet ...
from deepest backwood, furthest under ...'
And every minute his lorgnette
stays fixed and focused on a vision
which has recalled, without precision,
forgotten features. 'Can you say,
prince, who in that dark-red béret,
just there, is talking to the Spanish
ambassador?' In some surprise
the prince looks at him, and replies:
'Wait, I'll present you – but you banish
yourself too long from social life.'
'But tell me who she is.' 'My wife.'

XVIII

'You're married? No idea whatever . . .
Since when is this?' 'Two years or more.'
'To . . . ?' 'Larina.' 'Tatyana? never!'
'She knows you?' 'Why, we lived next door.'
So to his wife for presentation
the prince brings up his own relation
and friend Evgeny. The princess
gazes at him . . . and nonetheless,
however much her soul has faltered,
however strongly she has been
moved and surprised, she stays serene,
and nothing in her look is altered:
her manner is no less contained;
her bow, as calm and as restrained.

XIX

I don't mean that she never shivered,
paled, flushed, or lost composure's grip –
no, even her eyebrow never quivered,
she never even bit her lip.
However closely he inspected,
there was no trace to be detected
of the old Tatyana. Eugene tried
to talk to her, but language died.
How long he'd been here, was her query,
and where had he arrived from, not
from their own country? Then she shot
across to her consort a weary
regard, and slipped away for good, . . .
with Eugene frozen where he stood.

XX

Was she the Tanya he'd exhorted
in solitude, as at the start
of this our novel we reported,
in the far backwoods' deepest heart,
to whom, in a fine flow of preaching,
he had conveyed some moral teaching,
from whom he'd kept a letter, where
her heart had spoken, free as air,
untouched by trace of inhibition,
could it be she . . . or had he dreamed?
the girl he'd scorned in what he deemed
the modesty of her condition,
could it be she, who just had turned
away, so cool, so unconcerned?

XXI

Eugene forsakes the packed reception,
and home he drives, deep-sunk in thought.
By dreams now sad in their conception,
now sweet, his slumbers are distraught.
He wakes – and who is this who writes him?
Prince N. respectfully invites him
to a *soirée*. 'My God! to her! . . .
I'll go, I'll go!' – and in a stir
a swift, polite reply is written.
What ails him? he's in some strange daze!
what moves along the hidden ways
in one so slothful, so hard-bitten?
vexation? vainness? heavens above,
it can't be youth's distemper – love?

XXII

Once more he counts the hour-bells tolling,
once more he can't await the night;
now ten has struck, his wheels are rolling,
he drives there like a bird in flight.
he's up the steps, with heart a-quiver
led to the princess, all a-shiver,
finds her alone, and there they sit
some minutes long. The words won't fit
on Eugene's lips. In his dejection,
his awkwardness, he's hardly said
a single thing to her. His head
is lost in obstinate reflection;
and obstinate his look. But she
sits imperturbable, and free.

XXIII

Her husband enters, thus concluding
their unattractive *tête-à-tête;*
he and Onegin start alluding
to pranks and jokes of earlier date.
They laugh. The guests begin arriving.
Already now the talk was thriving
on modish malice, coarse of grain
but salt; near the princess a vein
of unaffectedly fantastic
invention sparkled, then gave way
to reasoned talk, no dull hearsay,
no deathless truths, nothing scholastic;
and no one's ear could take offence
at such vivacious, free good sense.

XXIV

High rank, of course, and fashion's glasses,
Saint Petersburg's fine flower was there —
the inevitable silly asses,
the faces met with everywhere;
ladies of riper years, delicious
in rose-trimmed bonnets, but malicious;
a girl or two, without a smile
to crack between them; for a while
one listened to a chief of mission
on state affairs; there was a wit,
a grey-haired, perfumed exquisite,
a joker in the old tradition,
acute and subtle — in a word
all that today we find absurd.

XXV

There, with epigrammatic neatness,
was one who raged and raged again,
against the tea's excessive sweetness,
the boring wives, the ill-bred men,
a novel, vague and superficial,
two sisters who'd received the initial,
the lies that in the press run rife,
the war, the snowfall, and his wife.

. . . .

XXVI

There was — —, so notorious
through baseness of the soul that he,
in albums, blunted the censorious
cartoonist-pencils of Saint-Priest;
another of the ball-dictators,
a fashion-plate for illustrators,
stood in the door, cherubic, mute,
frozen in his tight-fitting suit;
a far-flung traveller who was creaking
with foppery and too much starch,
set the guests smiling at his arch,
affected pose – and an unspeaking
unanimous exchange of looks
entered his sentence in the books.

XXVII

But my Eugene that night directed
his gaze at Tatyana alone –
not the plain, timorous, dejected
and lovelorn maiden whom he'd known,
but the unbending goddess-daughter
of Neva's proud imperial water,
the imperturbable princess.
We all resemble more or less
our Mother Eve: we're never falling
for what's been given us to take;
to his mysterious tree the snake
is calling us, for ever calling –
and once forbidden fruit is seen,
no paradise can stay serene.

XXVIII

In Tanya, what a transformation!
how well she'd studied her new role!
how soon the bounds of rank and station
had won her loyalty! What soul
would have divined the tender, shrinking
maiden in this superb, unthinking
lawgiver to the modish world?
Yet once for him her thoughts had whirled,
for him, at night, before the indulgence
of Morpheus had induced relief
she once had pined in girlish grief,
raised a dull eye to moon's refulgence,
and dreamt that she with him one day
jointly would tread life's humble way!

XXIX

Love tyrannises all the ages;
but youthful, virgin hearts derive
a blessing from its blasts and rages,
like fields in spring when storms arrive.
In passion's sluicing rain they freshen,
ripen, and find a new expression –
the vital force gives them the shoot
of sumptuous flowers and luscious fruit.
But when a later age has found us,
the climacteric of our life,
how sad the scar of passion's knife:
as when chill autumn rains surround us,
throw meadows into muddy rout,
and strip the forest round about.

XXX

Alas, Eugene beyond all query
is deep in love, just like a boy;
spends light and darkness in the dreary
brooding that is the lover's ploy.
Each day, despite the appeals of reason,
he drives up in and out of season
to her glass porch; pursues her round
close as a shadow on the ground;
and bliss for him is when he hotly
touches her hand, or throws a fur
around her neck, or when for her
he goes ahead and parts the motley
brigade of liveries in the hall,
or else lifts up a fallen shawl.

XXXI

But she refuses to perceive him,
even if he drops or pines away.
At home she'll equably receive him,
in others' houses she may say
a word or two, or stare unseeing,
or simply bow: within her being
coquettishness has got no trace —
the *grand monde* finds it out of place.
Meanwhile Onegin starts to languish:
she doesn't see, or doesn't mind;
Onegin wastes, you'd almost find
he's got consumption. In his anguish
some vote a doctor for the case,
others prescribe a watering-place.

XXXII

But go he won't: for him, a letter
fixing an early rendezvous
with his forefathers would seem better;
but she (for women, that's not new)
remains unmoved: still he's persistent,
active, and hopeful, and insistent:
his illness lends him courage and
to the princess, in his weak hand,
he sends a letter, penned with passion.
He deemed, in general, letters vain,
and rightly so, but now his pain
had gone in no uncertain fashion
past all endurance. You're referred
to Eugene's letter, word for word.

ONEGIN'S LETTER TO TATYANA

'I know it all: my secret ache
will anger you in its confession.
What scorn I see in the expression
that your proud glance is sure to take!
What do I want? what am I after,
stripping my soul before your eyes?
I know to what malicious laughter
my declaration may give rise!

'I noticed once, at our chance meeting,
in you a tender pulse was beating,
yet dared not trust what I could see.
I gave no rein to sweet affection;
what held me was my predilection,
my tedious taste for feeling free.
And then, to part us in full measure,
Lensky, that tragic victim, died . . .
From all sweet things that gave me pleasure,
since then my heart was wrenched aside;
freedom and peace, in substitution
for happiness, I sought, and ranged
unloved, and friendless, and estranged.
What folly! and what retribution!

'No, every minute of my days,
to see you, faithfully to follow,
watch for your smile, and catch your gaze
with eyes of love, with greed to swallow
your words, and in my soul to explore

your matchlessness, to seek to capture
its image, then to swoon before
your feet, to pale and waste . . . what rapture!

'But I'm denied this: all for you
I drag my footsteps hither, yonder;
I count each hour the whole day through;
and yet in vain ennui *I squander*
the days that doom has measured out.
And how they weigh! I know about
my span, that fortune's jurisdiction
has fixed; but for my heart to beat
I must wake up with the conviction
that somehow that same day we'll meet . . .

'I dread your stern regard surmising
in my petition an approach,
a calculation past despising —
I hear the wrath of your reproach.
How fearful, in and out of season
to pine away from passion's thirst,
to burn — and then by force of reason
to stem the bloodstream's wild outburst;
how fearful, too, is my obsession
to clasp your knees, and at your feet
to sob out prayer, complaint, confession,
and every plea that lips can treat;
meanwhile with a dissembler's duty
to cool my glances and my tongue,

to talk as if with heart unwrung,
and look serenely on your beauty! ...

'But so it is: I'm in no state
to battle further with my passion;
I'm yours, in a predestined fashion,
and I surrender to my fate.'

XXXIII

No answer comes. Another letter
he sends, a second, then a third.
No answer comes. He goes, for better
or worse, to a *soirée*. Unheard
she appears before him, grim and frozen.
No look, no word for him: she's chosen
to encase herself inside a layer
of Twelfth Night's chillest, iciest air.
To batten down their indignation
is all those stubborn lips desire!
Onegin looks with eyes of fire:
where are distress, commiseration?
No tearstains, nothing. Wrath alone
is graven on that face of stone.

XXXIV

Perhaps some secret apprehension
lest signs of casual weakness drew
her husband's or the world's attention . . .
Ah, all that my Onegin knew . . .
No hope! no hope! He leaves the revel,
wishes his madness to the devil,
drives home — and plunging deeper in,
once more renounces world and din.
And he remembers, in the quiet
of his own room, how cruel spleen
had once before, across the scene
of social buzz and modish riot,
tracked him, and put him in duress,
and locked him in a dark recess.

XXXV

Once more he turned to books, unchoosing,
devouring Gibbon and Rousseau,
Manzoni and Chamfort, perusing
Madame de Staël, Bichat, Tissot,
Herder, and even at times a Russian –
nothing was barred beyond discussion –
he read of course the sceptic Bayle
and all the works of Fontanelle –
almanacs, journals of reflection,
where admonitions are pronounced,
where nowadays I'm soundly trounced,
but where such hymns in my direction
were chanted, I remember when –
e sempre bene, gentlemen.

XXXVI

What happened? Though his eyes were reading,
his thoughts were on a distant goal:
desires and dreams and griefs were breeding
and swarming in his inmost soul.
Between the lines of text as printed,
his mind's eye focused on the hinted
purport of other lines; intense
was his absorption in their sense.
Legends, and mystical traditions,
drawn from a dim, warm-hearted past,
dreams of inconsequential cast,
rumours and threats and premonitions,
long, lively tales from wonderland,
or letters in a young girl's hand.

Then gradually upon sensation,
and thought, a sleepy numbness steals;
before his eyes, imagination
brings out its faro pack, and deals.
He sees: in slush, stretched out and keeping
motionless as one soundly sleeping
in bed, a young man, stiff and chilled;
he hears a voice: 'well, what? he's killed!'
And foes he sees, long-since forgotten,
a rogue, a slanderer, a poltroon,
young traitresses by the platoon,
comrades despised, and comrades rotten;
a country house – and *one* who still
sits there beside the window-sill!

XXXVIII

He got so used to this immersion,
he almost lost his mind, expired,
or joined us poets. His conversion
would have been all that we required!
It's true, the magnet-like attraction
of Russian verse, its force in action, –
my inept pupil, at that hour,
so nearly had them in his power.
Who could have looked the poet better,
as in the nook he'd sit alone
by blazing fireplace, and intone
Idol mio or *Benedetta*,
and on the flames let fall unseen
a slipper, or a magazine?

XXXIX

The days flew past; by now the season
in warmer airs was half dispersed.
He's neither died, nor lost his reason,
nor turned a poet. In the burst
of spring he lives, he's energetic;
he leaves one morning the hermetic
apartment where a double glaze
has kept him warm in chimney's blaze
while, marmot-like, he hibernated –
along the Neva in a sleigh,
past ice-blocks, blue and squared away,
he drives in brilliant sun; striated
along the street lies dirty snow;
and like an arrow from a bow

XL

over the slush, where is he chasing?
You've guessed before it all began:
to his Tatyana, yes, he's racing,
my strange, incorrigible man.
He goes inside, corpse-like of feature . . .
the hall's without a living creature,
the big room, further, not a cat.
He opens up a door. What's that
that strikes him with such force and meaning?
The princess, sitting peaked and wan,
alone, with no adornment on;
she holds a letter up, and leaning
cheek upon hand she softly cries
in a still stream that never dries.

XLI

Who in that flash could not have reckoned
her full account of voiceless pain?
Who in the princess for that second
would not have recognized again
our hapless Tanya! An emotion
of wild repentance and devotion
threw Eugene at her feet — she stirred,
and looked at him without a word,
without surprise or rage ... his laden,
his humbly suppliant approach,
his dull, sick look, his dumb reproach —
she sees it all. The simple maiden,
whose heart on dreams was wont to thrive,
in her once more has come alive.

XLII

Tatyana leaves Onegin kneeling,
looks at him with a steady gaze,
allows her hand, that's lost all feeling,
to meet his thirsty lips ... What daze,
what dream accounts for her distraction?
A pause of silence and inaction,
then quietly at lasts says she:
'Enough, stand up. It's now for me
to give you honest explanation.
Onegin, d'you recall the day
when in the park, in the *allée*
where fate had fixed our confrontation,
humbly I heard your lesson out?
Today it's turn and turn about.

XLIII

'For then, Onegin, I was younger,
and also prettier, I'll be bound,
what's more, I loved you; but my hunger,
what was it in your heart it found
that could sustain it? Only grimness;
for you, I think, the humble dimness
of lovelorn girls was nothing new?
But now – oh God! – the thought of you,
your icy look, your stern dissuasion,
freezes my blood . . . Yet all the same,
nothing you did gave cause for blame:
you acted well, that dread occasion,
you took an honourable part –
I'm grateful now with all my heart.

XLIV

'Then, in the backwoods, far from rumour
and empty gossip, you'll allow,
I'd nothing to attract your humour . . .
Why then do you pursue me now?
What cause has won me your attention?
Could it not be that by convention
I move in the *grand monde?* that rank,
and riches, and the wish to thank
my husband for his wounds in battle
earn us the favour of the Court?
that, for all this, my shame's report
would cause widespread remark and tattle,
and so in the *salons* could make
a tempting plume for you to take?

XLV

'I weep . . . In case there still should linger
your Tanya's image in your mind,
then know that your reproving finger,
your cold discourse, were less unkind —
if I had power to choose your fashion —
than this humiliating passion
and than these letters, and these tears.
At least you then showed for my years
respect, and mercy for my dreaming.
But now! what brings you to my feet?
What trifling could be more complete?
What power enslaves you, with your seeming
advantages of heart and brain,
to all that's trivial and inane?

XLVI

'To me, Onegin, all this glory
is tinsel on a life I hate;
this modish whirl, this social story,
my house, my evenings, all that state —
what's in them? All this loud parading,
and all this flashy masquerading,
the glare, the fumes in which I live,
this very day I'd gladly give,
give for a bookshelf, a neglected
garden, a modest home, the place
of our first meeting face to face,
and the churchyard where, new-erected,
a humble cross, in woodland gloom,
stands over my poor nurse's tomb.

XLVII

'Bliss was so near, so altogether
attainable! . . . But now my lot
is firmly cast. I don't know whether
I acted thoughtlessly or not:
you see, with tears and incantation
mother implored me; my sad station
made all fates look the same . . . and so
I married. I beseech you, go;
I know your heart: it has a feeling
for honour, a straightforward pride.
I love you (what's the use to hide
behind deceit or double-dealing?)
but I've become another's wife –
and I'll be true to him, for life.'

XLVIII

She went – and Eugene, all emotion,
stood thunder-struck. In what wild round
of tempests, in what raging ocean
his heart was plunged! A sudden sound,
the clink of rowels, met his hearing;
Tatyana's husband, now appearing . . .
But from the hero of my tale,
just at this crisis of his gale,
reader, we must be separating,
for long . . . for evermore. We've chased
him far enough through wild and waste.
Hurrah! let's start congratulating
ourselves on our landfall. It's true,
our vessel's long been overdue.

XLIX

Reader, I wish that, as we parted —
whoever you may be, a friend,
a foe — our mood should be warm-hearted.
Goodbye, for now we make an end.
Whatever in this rough confection
you sought — tumultuous recollection,
a rest from toil and all its aches,
or just grammatical mistakes,
a vivid brush, a witty rattle —
God grant that from this little book
for heart's delight, or fun, you took,
for dreams, or journalistic battle,
God grant you took at least a grain.
On this we'll part; goodbye again!

L

And my companion, so mysterious,
goodbye to you, my true ideal,
my task, so vivid and so serious
and yet so light. All that is real
and enviable for a poet,
in your pursuit I've come to know it:
oblivion of life's stormy ways,
sweet talk with friends. How many days
since, through the mist that dreams arise on,
young Tanya first appeared to me,
Onegin too — and there to see,
a free romance's far horizon,
still dim, through crystal's magic glass,
before my gaze began to pass.

LI

Of those who heard my opening pages
in friendly gatherings where I read,
as Sadi sang in earlier ages,
'some are far distant, some are dead'.
They've missed Eugene's completed etching.
But she who modelled for the sketching
of Tanya's image ... Ah, how great
the toll of those borne off by fate!
Blest he who's left the hurly-burly
of life's repast betimes, nor sought
to drain its beaker down, nor thought
of finishing its book, but early
has wished it an abrupt goodbye –
and, with my Eugene, so have I.

I–VIII

E. Onegin drives from Moscow to Nizhny Novgorod.

IX

– – – – – – – – – – – – – – – – – –
– – – – – – – – – – – – – before his eyes
Makaryev market hums and buzzes,
and seethes, and bursts with merchandise.
The Indian's brought here pearls like carrots,
the European – dubious clarets;
the steppeland breeder's come to town
with strings of horses (broken down),
and here are cards, the gamester's passion,
with handfuls of conniving dice;
the steppe landowner's brought his nice
ripe daughters, dressed in last year's fashion.
All's trade, and lies enough for two,
and noise, and general how d'you do.

X–XI

Boredom! . . .
Onegin travels to Astrakhan, and from there to the Caucasus.

XII

He sees proud Terek, magisterial,
gnaw the steep confines of its bed;
up here, an eagle planes, imperial,
a stag stands there with lowered head.
In cliff-shadow, a camel's lying;
through fields a Cherkess horse is flying;
round tents of a nomadic breed
the sheepflocks of the Kalmuck feed.
Far off loom the Caucasian masses;
their road is open. War has pried
its way through their age-old divide,
across their barriers and crevasses.
Arágva and Kurá have now
seen Russian tents upon their brow.

XIII

But soon, above his desert sector,
while foothills all around him press,
Beshtú, serrated old protector,
stands with Mashúk of the green dress,
Mashúk, the source of healing rivers;
about his streams, those charmed life-givers,
swarm the pale orders of the faint,
victims of battle's proud complaint,
of kidneys, or of Aphrodite;
some think their life is like a length
of thread, the waves will give it strength;
coquettes hope the débris of flighty
decades will wash right off; old men
want, for a trice, youth back again.

XIV

Inspired to embittered meditation,
amidst this pitiable brigade,
Onegin with commiseration
questions the smoking stream, dismayed
by mists of gloom that hold him under:
Why have I no chest-wound, I wonder?
Why, like that tax-farmer, can't I
be old and doddering? Or why
on earth can't I be paralytic,
like Tula's councillor, or if not
why couldn't I at least have got
a shoulder that's a touch arthritic?
Oh God, I'm young, I'm fresh, I'm strong –
and I've got boredom, all day long.

Onegin then visits Tauris

XV

– – – – – – – – – – – – – – – – – –
– – – – – – – – – – – – – – – – – –
– – – – – – – – – – – – – – – – – –
– – – – – – – – – – – – – – – – – –

scene, sacred to the imagination,
of Mithridates' suicide;
here Pylad and Orestes vied,
and Mickiéwicz, at the inspiration
of cliffs that beetle more and more,
recalled his Lithuanian shore.

XVI

Coasts of Tauris, seen at dawning
as first I saw you, from shipboard,
by light of moon that challenged morning,
your beauty stood to be adored,
you radiated bridal splendour:
against the sky, pellucid-tender,
your mountains raised their gleaming breasts;
your patchwork of ravines and crests
and trees and hamlets kept unfolding.
And there, in Tartar huts ... what fire,
what sad enchantments of desire,
awoke in me, and soon were holding
my all too ardent bosom fast!
My Muse, you must forget the past.

XVII

Whatever feelings may have smarted
inside me then, they fled away:
they're all transmuted or departed ...
peace to you, storms of yesterday!
Then my imagination ordered
deserts, and billows pearly-bordered,
sea-tumult, summits craggy-browed,
with my ideal, the maiden proud,
and sufferings quite beyond redeeming ...
and yet new seasons always bring
new visions; humbled is my spring
with its inebriated dreaming,
and, as a poet, I've topped up
the water-quotient in my cup.

XVIII

Today, I'll buy a different ticket:
I like a sandy hillside track,
a hut, two ash-trees and a wicket,
some fencing with a broken back,
a sky where greyish clouds are flying,
a threshing-floor where straw is lying,
and in the shade of willow-trees
a pond where ducklings take their ease;
now balalaikas are my pleasure,
the trepák with its tipsy clop
outside the village drinking-shop.
I live for quiet, what I treasure
as my ideal is the housewife –
and cabbage soup, and my own life.

XIX

Not long ago, in rainy weather,
I turned into the cattle-yard . . .
Rubbish! Too prosy altogether,
the Flemish School's diffuse regard!
Was I, when I'd my prime to impel me –
O Bakhchisaray Fountain, tell me –
as dull as this, or was such trash
suggested by your endless plash
as, silent, instant procreator
of my Zaréma, I stood there?
Those halls, deserted, sumptuous, bare,
Onegin entered three years later,
when, in my wake, he chanced to be
in the same lands, and thought of me.

XX

My home at that time was Odessa
the dusty, whose clear sky prevails,
where an abundant trade's possessor
is ever busy hoisting sails.
There Europe blows on all the breezes,
life glitters with the South, and pleases
as shiftingly its hues unfold.
The speech of Italy, land of gold,
rings in the merry streets, the places
where lordly Slavs and Frenchmen walk,
where Spaniards and Armenians talk,
Moldavians, heaviest of races,
and Greeks, and Egypt's sons are there,
and Moralí, half-pay Corsair.

XXI

Odessa in sonorous fashion
our friend Tumansky set to rhyme,
and yet it was with too much passion
that he looked on it at that time.
He arrived, and like a regular poet
took his lorgnette to get to know it,
and roamed the shore alone, and then
Odessa's gardens with his pen
he sang in verses that enchanted.
So far, so good, and yet in fact
all round is steppeland's naked tract;
and only recent toil has planted
young boughs that on dog-days are made
to offer a conscripted shade.

XXII

Where did my rambling story leave you?
Odessa, town of dust, I said.
I well could say, and not deceive you,
Odessa, town of mud, instead.
Five or six weeks, by disposition
of squally Zeus, bring a condition
each year of stoppage and of flood
and foundering-up in thickest mud.
Houses are two feet in, pedestrians
daren't ford the street without a stilt
to take them safely through the silt:
bogged carriages, engulfed equestrians –
from drozhky's shafts poor horse is gone,
and straining ox must carry on.

XXIII

But stones are being hammered, paving
will soon be ringing in the street,
and soon the town will be for saving
as with a base of armoured sheet.
And yet, in waterlogged Odessa,
we still must reckon with no less a
deficiency of – what d'you think?
We're short of water fit to drink.
There's much work to be done ... but really
is it so grave for you and me
when wine's imported customs-free?
And southern sun, and sea ... Ideally
what more could we desire, my friend?
Blest country, fortunate world's end!

XXIV

Hardly from shipboard had exploded
the thunder of the sunrise gun,
than seaward down the steep-eroded
littoral I'd be on the run.
And then, with hookah incandescent,
my thoughts by brine made effervescent,
like Moslems in their paradise
I'd drink, complete with grounds and spice,
an Eastern coffee. Time for walking.
Already open is the blest
Casino; cups are clinked with zest;
on balcony, still tired from chalking,
the marker plies his broom; below
two merchants have just said 'hello.'

XXV

The square has swarmed. You look about it —
it comes to life; and like a game
they run, on business or without it,
mostly on business all the same.
Offspring of risk and circumspection,
the merchant goes on an inspection
of flags, to see if heaven's consigned
him sails he knows. He wants to find
each cargo that's just been imported
and registered in quarantine.
Has the wine shipment yet been seen?
What plagues, what fires have been reported?
Is there no famine, or no war,
or nothing new like that in store?

XXVI

We, carefree children on the roister
amidst the *affairé* merchants, had
no worry but to await the oyster
brought from the shores of Tsaregrad.
Oysters? They've just come in. Delicious!
Away the young have flown, lubricious
gourmets, to gulp from the seashells
those plump, live hermits in their cells,
splashed with a drop of lemon. Babel
of argument – and a light wine
that Automne from his cellar-shrine,
ever obliging, brings to table;
the hours fly past, and the grim bill
invisibly grows grimmer still.

XXVII

But the blue evening's dimmed; no later
it's Opera-time, and off we go
for Rossini, arch-captivator,
Europe's spoilt Orpheus, is on show.
To scowling critics inattentive,
always the same, always inventive,
he pours out melodies that hiss,
that kindle like a youthful kiss,
that flow, that burn, that move and trouble,
all sensuous languor, flaming love,
like Aÿ shooting out above
in fizzing flood and golden bubble . . .
But dare I, gentlemen, d'you think,
equate do-re-mi-sol with drink?

XXVIII

Does that exhaust the fascinations?
Are there no fields for glass to explore?
What about back-stage assignations,
or prima donna, or ballet corps?
The box where, brilliant apparition
compact of languor and ambition,
there sits the merchant's youthful wife,
hemmed by a throng of slaves-for-life?
She listens, heedful yet unheedful,
to cavatinas and to prayers
and jokes and flattery mixed in layers . . .
meanwhile her spouse, out of his needful
nap in a corner, shouts 'Encore!'
and yawns – and starts to again snore.

XXIX

Now the finale roars; spectators
forsake the hall in noisy flight;
the square is packed with celebrators
by lantern-light or by starlight;
happy Ausonia's sons are singing
a light, gay aria that keeps ringing
in memory without conscious leave –
while we boom the recitative.
It's late. Odessa's quietly dreaming;
breathless and warm and deeply still
the night. The moon's above the sill,
and a thin veil, pellucid-gleaming,
enfolds the sky. Silence all round;
the Black Sea makes the only sound . . .

XXX
And so I lived then in Odessa . . .

THE BRONZE HORSEMAN
A Petersburg Tale

FOREWORD

The event described in this tale is based on fact. The
details of the flood are borrowed from newspapers of
the time. The curious can consult the account compiled
by V. I. Berkh.

INTRODUCTION

Upon the brink of the wild stream
He stood, and dreamt a mighty dream.
He gazed far off. Near him the spreading
river poured by; with flood abeam,
alone, a flimsy skiff was treading.
Scattered along those shores of bog
and moss were huts of blackened log,
the wretched fisher's squalid dwelling;
forests, impervious in the fog
to hidden suns, all round were telling
their whispered tale.

     And so thought He:
'From here, proud Sweden will get warning;
just here is where a city'll be
founded to stop our foes from scorning;
here Nature destines us to throw
out over Europe a window;
to stand steadfast beside the waters;
across waves unknown to the West,
all flags will come, to be our guest –
and we shall feast in spacious quarters.'

A century went by – a young
city, of Northern lands the glory
and pride, from marsh and overhung
forest arose, storey on storey:
where, earlier, Finland's fisher sank –
of Nature's brood the most downhearted –
alone on the low-lying bank,
his ropy net in the uncharted
current, today, on brinks that hum
with life and movement, there have come
enormous mansions that are justling
with graceful towers; and vessels here
from earth's extremities will steer
until the rich quayside is bustling.
Nevá now sports a granite face;
bridges are strung across her waters;
in darkly verdant garden-quarters
her isles have vanished without trace;
old Moscow's paled before this other
metropolis; it's just the same
as when a widowed Empress-Mother
bows to a young Tsaritsa's claim.

I love you, Peter's own creation;
I love your stern, your stately air,
Nevá's majestical pulsation,
the granite that her quaysides wear,
your railings with their iron shimmer,
your pensive nights in the half-gloom,
translucent twilight, moonless glimmer,
when, sitting lampless in my room,
I write and read; when, faintly shining,

the streets in their immense outlining
are empty, given up to dreams;
when Admiralty's needle gleams;
when not admitting shades infernal
into the golden sky, one glow
succeeds another, and nocturnal
tenure has one half-hour to go;
I love your brutal winter, freezing
the air to so much windless space;
by broad Nevá the sledges breezing;
brighter than roses each girl's face;
the ball, its brilliance, din, and malice;
bachelor banquets and the due
hiss of the overflowing chalice,
and punch's radiance burning blue.
I love it when some warlike duty
livens the Field of Mars, and horse
and foot impose on that concourse
their monolithic brand of beauty;
above the smooth-swaying vanguard
victorious, tattered flags are streaming,
on brazen helmets light is gleaming,
helmets that war has pierced and scarred.
I love the martial detonation,
the citadel in smoke and roar,
when the North's Empress to the nation
has given a son for empire, or
when there's some new triumph in war
victorious Russia's celebrating;
or when Nevá breaks the blue ice,
sweeps it to seaward, slice on slice,

and smells that days of spring are waiting.

    Metropolis of Peter, stand,
steadfast as Russia, stand in splendour!
Even the elements by your hand
have been subdued and made surrender;
let Finland's waves forget the band
of hate and bondage down the ages,
nor trouble with their fruitless rages
Peter the Great's eternal sleep!

    A fearful time there was: I keep
its memory fresh in retrospection . . .
My friends, let me turn up for you
the dossiers of recollection.
Grievous the tale will be, it's true . . .

(29 October)

PART ONE

    On Petrograd, the darkened city,
November, chill and without pity,
blasted; against its noble brink
Nevá was splashing noisy billows;
its restless mood would make one think
of sufferers on their restless pillows.
The hour was late and dark; the rain
angrily lashed the window-pane,
the wind blew, pitifully shrieking.
From house of friends, about this time,
young Evgeny came home . . .

                            My rhyme
selects this name to use in speaking

of our young hero. It's a sound
I like; my pen has long been bound
in some way with it; further naming
is not required, though lustre flaming
in years gone by might have lit on
his forebears, and perhaps their story
under Karamzin's pen had shone,
resounding to the nation's glory;
but now by all, both high and low,
it's quite forgotten. Our hero
lives in Kolomna, has employment
in some bureau, tastes no enjoyment
of wealth or fashion's world, and no
regret for tales of long ago.

So Evgeny came home and, shaking
his greatcoat, got undressed for bed –
but lay long hours awake, his head
with various thoughts disturbed and aching.
What did he think about? The fact
that he was penniless; that packed
mountains of work must be surmounted
to earn him freedom, fame, and ease;
that wit and money might be counted
to him from God; and that one sees
fellows on permanent vacation,
dull-witted, idle, in whose station
life runs as smooth as in a dream;
that he'd served two years altogether . . .
And he thought also that the weather
had got no gentler; that the stream

was rising, ever higher lifting;
that soon the bridges might be shifting;
that maybe from Parasha he
would be cut off, two days or three.

These were his dreams. And a great sadness
came over him that night; he wished
the raindrops with less raging madness
would lash the glass, that the wind swished
less drearily . . .

                    At last his failing
eyes closed in sleep. But look, the gloom
of that foul-weather night is paling,
and a weak daylight fills the room . . .
A dreadful day it was!
                    All night
Nevá against the gales to seaward
had battled, but been blown to leeward
by their ungovernable might . . .
That morning, on the quayside, fountains
of spray held an admiring crowd,
that pressed to watch the watery mountains,
the foaming waves that roared so loud.
But now, blocked by the headwinds blowing
in from the Gulf, Nevá turned back,
in sullen, thunderous fury flowing,
and flooded all the islands; black,
still blacker grew the day; still swelling,
Nevá exploded, raging, yelling,
in kettle-like outbursts of steam –

until, mad as a beast, the stream
pounced on the city. From its path
everyone fled, and all around
was sudden desert ... At a bound
cellars were under inundation,
canals leapt rails, forgot their station –
and Triton-Petropol surfaced
with waters lapping round his waist.

    Siege and assault! The waves, malicious,
like thieves, burst in through windows; vicious
rowboats, careering, smash the panes;
stalls are engulfed; piteous remains,
débris of cabins, roofing, boarding,
wares that a thrifty trade's been hoarding,
poor household goods, dashed all astray,
bridges the storm has snatched away,
and scooped-up coffins, helter-skelter
swim down the streets!

                  All sense alike
God's wrath, and wait for doom to strike.
Everything's ruined: bread and shelter!
and where to find them?

                  That deathlike,
that frightful year, Tsar Alexander
still ruled in glory. He came out
on the balcony, in grief, in doubt,
and said: 'A Tsar is no commander
against God's elements.' Deep in thought
he gazed with sorrow and confusion,
gazed at the wreck the floods had wrought.
The city squares gave the illusion

of lakes kept brimming to profusion
by torrent-streets. The palace stood
sad as an island in the ocean.
And then the Tsar spoke out, for good
or evil set in farflung motion
his generals on their dangerous way
along those streets of boisterous waters
to save the people in their quarters,
drowning, unhinged by terror's sway.

    And then in Peter's square, where lately
a corner-mansion rose, and stately
from its high porch, on either side,
caught as in life, with paws suspended,
two lions, sentry-like, attended –
perched up on one, as if to ride,
arms folded, motionless, astride,
hatless, and pale with apprehension,
Evgeny sat. His fear's intention
not for himself, he never knew
just how the greedy waters grew,
how at his boots the waves were sucking,
how in his face the raindrops flew;
or how the stormwind, howling, bucking,
had snatched his hat away. His view
was fixed in darkest desperation,
immobile, on a single spot.
Mountainous, from the perturbation
down in the depths, the waves had got
on their high horses, raging, pouncing;
the gale blew up, and, with it, bouncing
wreckage ... Oh, God, oh God! for there –

close to the seashore – almost where
the Gulf ran in, right on the billow –
a fence, untouched by paint, a willow,
a flimsy cottage; *there* were they,
a widow and his dream, her daughter,
Parasha . . . or perhaps he may
have dreamt it all? Fickle as water,
our life is as dreamlike as smoke –
at our expense, fate's private joke.
As if by sorcery enchanted,
high on the marble fixed and planted,
he can't dismount! And all about
is only water. Looking out,
with back turned to him, on the retching
waves of Nevá in their wild course
from his fast summit, arm outstretching,
the Giant rides on his bronze horse.

(30 October)

PART TWO

But by now, tired of helter-skelter
ruin and sheer rampaging, back
Nevá was flowing, in its track
admiring its own hideous welter;
its booty, as it made for shelter,
it slung away. With his grim crew
so any robber chief will do;
bursting his way into a village,
he'll hack and thrust and snatch and pillage;
rape, havoc, terror, howl and wail!

Then, loaded down with loot, and weary –
fear of pursuers makes them leery –
the robbers take the homeward trail
and as they flee they scatter plunder.

So, while the waters fell asunder,
the road came up. And fainting, pale,
in hope and yearning, fear and wonder,
Evgeny hurries at full steam
down to the scarcely falling stream.
And yet, still proud, and still exulting,
the waves, still furious and insulting,
boiled as if over flames alight;
they still were lathered, foaming, seething
and deeply the Nevá was breathing
just like a horse flown from a fight.
Evgeny looks: a skiff is waiting –
Godsent – he rushes, invocating
the ferryman, who without a care
for just a few copecks quite gladly
agrees to take him, though still madly
the floods are boiling everywhere.
The boatman fought the agonising
billows like an experienced hand;
the cockboat with its enterprising
crew was quite ready for capsizing
at any moment – but dry land
at last it gained.

                              Evgeny, tearful,
rushes along the well-known ways
towards the well-known scene. His gaze
finds nothing it can grasp: too fearful

the sight! before him all is drowned,
or swept away, or tossed around;
cottages are askew, some crumbled
to sheer destruction, others tumbled
off by the waves; and all about,
as on a field of martial rout,
bodies lie weltered. Blankly staring,
Evgeny, uncomprehending, flies,
faint from a torment past all bearing,
runs to where fate will meet his eyes,
fate whose unknown adjudication
still waits as under seal of wax.
And now he's near his destination
and here's the Gulf, here . . . in his tracks
Evgeny halts . . . the house . . . where ever?
he goes back, he returns. He'd never . . .
he looks . . . he walks . . . he looks again:
here's where their cottage stood; and then
here was the willow. Gates were standing
just here – swept off, for sure. But where's
the cottage gone? Not understanding,
he walked round, full of boding cares,
he talked to himself loud and gruffly,
and then he struck his forehead roughly
and laughed and laughed.
                              In deepest night
the city trembled at its plight:
long time that day's events were keeping
the citizenry all unsleeping
as they rehearsed them.
                              Daylight's ray

fell out of tired, pale clouds to play
over a scene of calm – at dawning
yesterday's hell had left no trace.
The purple radiance of the morning
had covered up the dire event.
All in its previous order went.
Upon highways no longer flowing,
people as everyday were going
in cold indifference, and the clerk
left where he'd sheltered in the dark
and went to work. The daring bosses
of commerce, unperturbed, explore
Nevá's inroads upon their store,
and plan to take their heavy losses
out on their neighbour. From backyards
boats are removed.

              That bard of bards,
Count Khvostov, great poetic master,
begins to sing Nevá's disaster
in unforgettable ballades.

    But spare, I pray you, spare some pity
for my poor, poor Evgeny, who
by the sad happenings in the city
had wits unhinged. Still the halloo
of tempest and Nevá was shrieking
into his ear; pierced through and through
by frightful thoughts, he roamed unspeaking;
some nightmare held him in its thrall.
A week went by, a month – and all
the time he never once was seeking
his home. That small deserted nook,

its lease expired, his landlord took
for a poor poet. His possessions
Evgeny never went to claim.
Soon to the world and its professions
a stranger, all day long he came
and went on foot, slept by the water;
scraps thrown from windows of the quarter
his only food; always the same,
his clothes wore out to shreds. Malicious
children would stone him; he received
from time to time the coachman's vicious
whiplash, for he no more perceived
which way was which, or what direction
led where; he never seemed to know
where he was going, he was so
plunged in tumult of introspection.
And so his life's unhappy span
he eked out – neither beast nor man –
not this, nor that – not really living
nor yet a ghost . . .
                          He slept one night
by the Nevá. Summer was giving
its place to autumn. Full of spite,
a bad wind blew. In mournful fight
against the embankment, waves were
        splashing,
their crests on the smooth steps were smashing
for all the world like suppliant poor
at some hard-hearted judge's door.
Evgeny woke. Raindrops were falling
in midnight gloom; the wind was calling

piteously – on it, far off, hark,
the cry of sentries in the dark . . .
Evgeny rose, and recollection
brought up past horrors for inspection;
he stood in haste, walked off from there,
then halted, and began to stare
in silence, with an insensately
wild look of terror on his face.
He was beside the pillared, stately
front of a mansion. In their place,
caught as in life, with paws suspended,
two lions, sentry-like, attended,
and there, above the river's course,
atop his rock, fenced-off, defended
on his dark summit, arm extended,
the Idol rode on his bronze horse.

    Evgeny shuddered. Thoughts were hatching
in frightful clarity. He knew
that spot, where floods ran raging through –
where waves had massed, voracious, snatching,
a riot-mob, vindictive, grim –
the lions, and the square, and him
who, motionless and without pity,
lifted his bronze head in the gloom,
whose will, implacable as doom,
had chosen seashore for his city.
Fearful he looked in that half-light!
Upon his forehead, what a might
of thought, what strength of concentration!
what fire, what passion, and what force

are all compact in that proud horse!
He gallops – to what destination?
On the cliff-edge, O lord of fate,
was it not you, O giant idol,
who, pulling on your iron bridle,
checked Russia, made her rear up straight?

    Around the hero's plinth of granite
wretched Evgeny, in a daze,
wandered, and turned a savage gaze
on the autocrat of half the planet.
A steely pressure gripped his chest.
His brow on the cold railing pressed,
over his eyes a mist was lowering,
and through his heart there ran a flame;
his blood was seething; so he came
to stand before the overpowering
image, with teeth and fists again
clenched as if some dark force possessed him.
'Take care,' he whisperingly addressed him,
'you marvel-working builder, when . . .'
He shivered with bitter fury, then
took headlong flight. He had the impression
that the grim Tsar, in sudden race
of blazing anger, turned his face
quietly and without expression . . .
and through the empty square he runs,
but hears behind him, loud as guns
or thunderclap's reverberation,
ponderous hooves in detonation
along the shuddering roadway –

as, lighted by the pale moon-ray,
one arm stretched up, on headlong course,
after him gallops the Bronze Rider,
after him clatters the Bronze Horse.
So all night long, demented strider
wherever he might turn his head –
everywhere gallops the Bronze Rider
pursuing him with thunderous tread.

And from then on, if he was chancing
at any time to cross that square,
a look of wild distress came glancing
across his features; he would there
press hand to heart, in tearing hurry,
as if to chase away a worry;
take his worn cap off; never raise
up from the ground his distraught gaze,
but sidle off.

A small isle rises
close to the foreshore. Now and then,
a fisher moors alongside, when
late from his catch, with nets and prizes,
and cooks his poor meal on the sand;
or some official comes to land,
out for a Sunday's pleasure-boating,
on the wild islet. Not a blade
of grass is seen. There, gaily floating,
the floods had washed up as they played
a flimsy cottage. Above water
it showed up like a bush, all black –
last spring they moved it. The small quarter,

empty, was shipped away, all rack
and ruin. Near it, my dim-witted
my mad Evgeny there they found . . .
His cold corpse in that self-same ground
to God's good mercy they committed.

(31 October 1833: Boldino, 5 past 5)